Spelling Stations Teacher's Guide

Written by Abigail Steel and Lisa Holt

Contents – Platform Two

Introduction 4-10

Week 1 - Ready to Depart
Platform One Review............. 11-14

Week 2 - On Track
Platform One Review............. 15-18

Week 3 - Huge Bridge
　　-ge, **-dge** /j/ 20-22

Week 4 - Magic Gym
　　ge, **gi**, **gy** /j/ 23-25

Week 5 - Ice City
　　ce, **ci**, **cy** /s/ 26-28

Week 6 - Knitted Gnomes
　　kn, **gn** /n/ 29-31

Week 7 - Wrinkly Writer
　　wr /r/ 32-34

Week 8 - Little Apples
　　–le 35-37

Week 9 - Camel Hospital
　　–el, **–al** 38-40

Week 10 - Pencil Stencil
　　–il 41-43

Week 11 - Dry July
　　–y /igh/.......................... 44-46

Week 12 - Baby Bunnies
　　–ies 47-49

Week 13 - Happy Happier
　　-ing, **-ed**, **-er**, **-est** 50-52

Week 14 - Stripy Hiker
　　-ing, **-ed**, **-er**, **-est**, **-y** 53-55

Week 15 - Humming Runner
　　-ing, **-ed**, **-er**, **-est**, **-y** 56-58

Week 16 - Wild Plant
　　Tricky Words 59-60

Week 17 - Small Stall
　　all, **al** /or/ 61-63

Week 18 - Honey Love
　　o /u/ 64-66

Week 19 - Donkey Valley
　　-ey /ee/ 67-69

Week 20 - Quality Watches
　　a /o/ after **qu** and **w** .. 70-72

Week 21 - Warm Workshop
　　ar /or/after **w**
　　or /er/after **w** 73-75

Week 22 - Treasure Measure
　　s /zh/ 76-78

Week 23 - Lovely Refreshment
　　-ly, **-ment**............. 79-81

Week 24 - Careful! Darkness!
　　–ful, **–less**, **–ness** 82-84

Week 25 - Don't run!
Contractions.......................85-87

Week 26 - Tom's Ticket
Possessive apostrophes
(singular nouns) 88-90

Week 27 - Action Station
　　–tion........................91-93

Week 28 - Blue Sea (Blew See)
Homophones and
near homophones............ 94-96

Week 29 - Busy People
Tricky Words 97-98

Week 30 - High Speed
Platform One and
Platform Two Review...... 99-100

Appendices................. 101-120

Introduction

Letterland Spelling Stations can be used with any curriculum, however, this guide covers the statutory requirements for Spelling in the National Curriculum for English at Key Stage 1, Year 2 (England).

By the time children embark on *Spelling Stations – Platform Two* they are likely to have mastered the basics of English spelling. Most children are able to think about the word they want to write and then spell it, either by remembering the way it looks if they have seen it before and are familiar with it, or by allocating letters to the sounds they can hear through the word. However, there are two main difficulties encountered at this point in the learning and development of spelling skills:

The first is that many words are not spelt 'the way they sound'. There are sometimes multiple spelling options for each sound. For example, if children want to spell **eight**, they can hear the sounds /ai/ and /t/ but the /ai/ sound can be represented by the following letter patterns in words: **ay**, **ai**, **a_e**, **a**, **eigh** or **ey**. If children have never previously seen the word **eight** written down or been explicitly taught the spelling of **eight**, they won't know which letters to use and may write **ayt** or **ait** instead.

The second difficulty is that as children get older, the quantity and complexity of vocabulary they encounter through speaking, listening and reading increases. Of course, this is hugely positive as we want children to learn and use as wide a vocabulary as possible, but the challenge comes when we cannot teach the spellings of new words quickly enough! This can have one of two effects on young writers – they either use their expanding vocabulary but spell lots of words incorrectly, or they don't use the words they know because they are fearful of spelling them wrong.

There is no short cut to learning which way words are spelt. Children require lots of practice with Word Banks, looking at spelling patterns and putting the words into context. Learning about spelling rules helps children become more aware of when and why words are spelt the way they are.

Research has shown that using a mnemonic system (an aide to memory) is a highly successful way of embedding spelling in children's long-term memories.

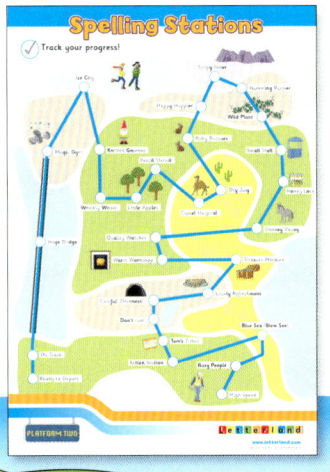

Letterland Spelling Stations uses several effective mnemonic strategies to embed spelling. The train station names provide an association for the linked banks of words and spelling rules. Each week has a station name and image associated with it. By remembering the station name, children have a visual clue to help them unlock the words of the week rather than simply having to remember an abstract list.

Download a **free map** of your journey to track your progress from:

www.letterland.com/information/downloads

How to use *Letterland Spelling Stations*

Letterland Spelling Stations is designed to guide you step-by-step as you teach your children to spell. You can follow the lessons as they are or you can tailor the lessons to suit your children and your timetable.

Make the lessons engaging

To be able to spell confidently, children need to be able to recall which spelling patterns are in words. By making the lessons fun, you will help to make learning memorable. It is therefore worth getting 'on board' with the theme of Spelling Stations in its entirety. You could put on a ticket inspector's hat at the start of each lesson and blow a whistle to show you are ready to start. You could even ask children to line up before the lesson and then board the train by taking their seats in the class.

A step-by-step approach

At the start of each lesson, **review previous learning** by asking children to recall the rule, or some of the words, they learned about in the previous lesson. If they struggle, you could support them by reminding them of the station name to prompt their memory. Don't spend too long on this but if you are concerned that the learning may not be embedded, then make an observational note that you will need to return to the previous lesson for further consolidation or look to the other Letterland programmes, such as *Letterland Phonics* or *Letterland Grammar* to consolidate learning.

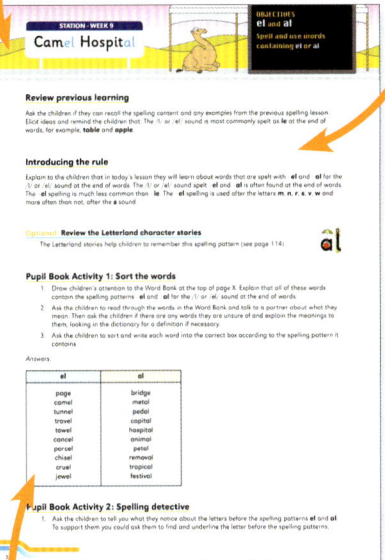

Next, move on to the lesson you are going to teach and introduce it by telling the children **the rule** and providing some examples.

Use the lesson plans to guide the children through the **activities** in the *Spelling Stations Pupil Book*. You may wish to divide the class, allowing more confident children to **work independently** through the activities (especially once they are familiar with the activity styles) while you focus your attention on supporting less confident children.

With a **supported group**, you may wish to complete each activity in the *Pupil Book* as a whole group, providing detailed instruction for the children in the group to work at the same pace.

Always have a **dictionary** to hand to be able to provide accurate definitions of the vocabulary used in the lessons and any additional vocabulary that may be raised. Activities in the *Pupil Book* such as 'Picture Match' and 'Complete the passage' are designed to highlight the meanings of the words in the Word Bank.

Remind children to pay careful attention to the letters in the words. Activities like 'Anagrams' and 'Word search' are designed to encourage children to notice and use the correct spellings.

You may wish to pause the lesson at a mid-point to discuss the answers to earlier activities in the *Pupil Book*. This can work well to identify any misconceptions that could be missed as the lesson progresses. Alternatively try to find some time towards the end of the lesson to review the activities and ask children to present to the class some of their answers in a collaborative feedback plenary.

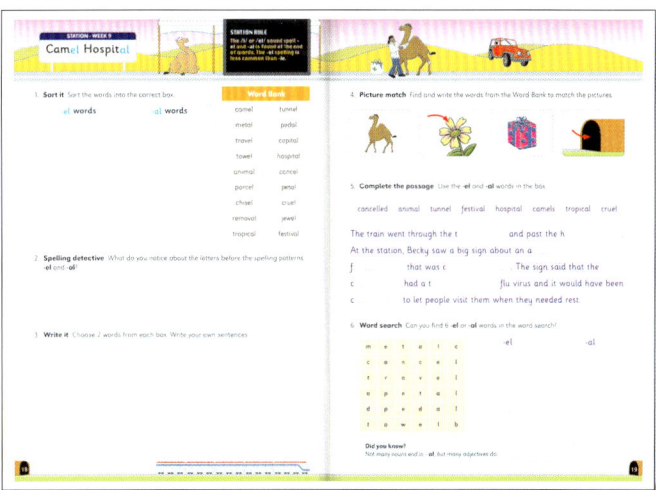

Teaching time: 2 x 30 minute sessions per week

The teaching week is divided into two parts. Each part should take around 20-30 minutes. Extention activities and optional games are provided that may extend the time somewhat if used.
See pages 106-111.

Assessment

As part of your weekly routine (generally a Friday activity), spellings should be assessed. To stop this being 'the dreaded test', introduce the idea of **Spelling Stations!**

Each child should have a copy of *Spelling Stations Ticket Book - Platform Two*. Each week they will be tested on the words from **one ticket**. Children will have covered the spelling patterns in class in their *Pupil Book*. Children should be encouraged to revise the spellings in the *Spelling Stations Ticket Book* at home with a parent/carer.

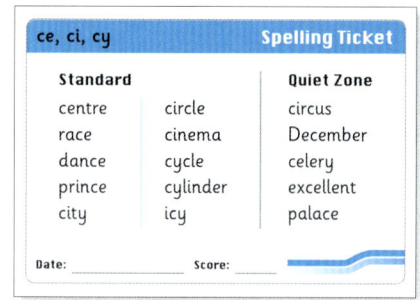

Teacher: At the start of the spelling test, you could say: **"Spelling Stations - Tickets Please!"** You could blow a whistle to signify the start and end of the test, or even put on a hat and pretend to be a ticket inspector.

Teacher: Collect in the *Spelling Stations Ticket Books*.

Teacher: Read out the 'Standard' Word Bank and sentences from the Assessment section of the *Teacher's Guide* to the children slowly. Repeat.

Students: Write their test answers in their own exercise book, or on a separate sheet of paper.

Teacher: Read out the 3-6 further 'Quiet Zone' words to spell for those in the class that need more of a spelling challenge. Remind the other children that they are in the 'Quiet Zone' and must stay quiet to help the other children concentrate.

Teacher: Collect all the students' answers to be marked.

(Option) Children check their own answers against their *Ticket Books*.

Teacher: Mark the papers and keep a record of the spelling scores on the sheets provided or your own class record (pages 103-104).

Teacher: Fill in the date (or use a date stamp) in each childs *Spelling Stations Ticket Book* and their score. Return marked Spelling Tests to your students. Ask them to look at any errors they have made and write those words again in the space provided **on the back of their Spelling Ticket** so they (and their parents) have a record of how they are getting on with their spellings.

Extension Option

To extend the assessment activity and provide further challenge, you could use the sentences from the Assessment section for full sentence dictations by reading them slowly and pausing after every few words to give children time to write down the full sentences.

Differentiation

Children learn in different ways and develop at different paces. *Letterland Spelling Stations* addresses this by providing a range of aural, visual and kinesthetic targeted spelling activities that embrace different learning styles. Differentiation opportunities are woven throughout so children are appropriately supported yet actively encouraged to stretch further. *Letterland Spelling Stations* is designed to be used with your whole class with built-in ways to accommodate below year group level spellers and students whose first language is not English, as well as those who are spelling above age-related expectations.

You will expect most students to learn the Standard list of 10-12 words per week, and the high achieving students to learn 15-18 words (both Standard and Quiet Zone). However, you may discretely advise some students which portion of the list he or she is responsible for learning. For example, you could limit a student to only being expected to spell 5 Standard Words. They fully participate in class activities but are evaluated primarily on assigned words.

Vocabulary discussion is particularly useful for new English language children (ELL) with the following adaptations:

- Include discussion of word meanings for **all words**.
- Involve ELL students in providing examples and finishing sentence stems after a few native speakers have modelled this process for a particular word.
- Guide your students in finding words with the same meaning in their first language through online translation sites.
- Because many languages have roots in the same languages, cognates can be found that are similarly spelt or pronounced in English and other languages.
- For students who are well below age-related expectations in reading and spelling, intervention at their instructional level is important.

Games

There are some activities and games provided at the back of this guide (pages 106-111). These are optional and can be used at any time to consolidate learning. Each game is 'train themed' so your class can really embrace the idea of Spelling Stations!

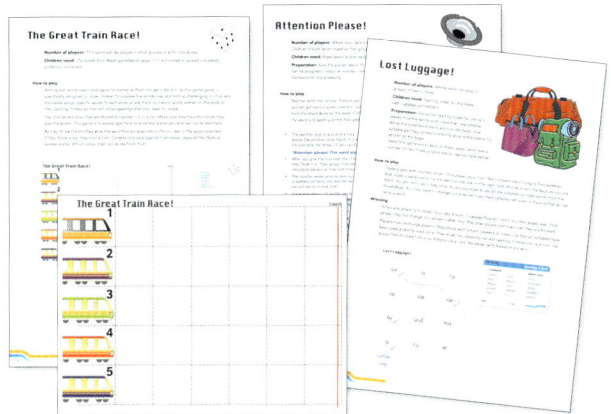

Full literacy support with Letterland

As a further source of reinforcement links are provided throughout the *Letterland Spelling Stations Teacher's Guide* to the *Letterland Phonics* character stories and the *Letterland Grammar* analogies.

Letterland covers all the curriculum requirements for literacy development including spelling, phonics and grammar. The resources we offer can be used independently of each other or together. **The uniting factor of all our materials is that the stories and analogies engage students leading to long term retention of concepts. Letterland is a child-friendly land of learning.**

For more information about *Letterland Phonics* or *Letterland Grammar*, see pages 112-118.

Pupil Resources

Spelling Stations Pupil Book - Platform Two

Each child should have a copy of the *Spelling Stations Pupil Book*. The book contains 30 double-page spreads, equivalent to two 20 minute sessions of activities per week. It covers the statutory requirements for Spelling in the National Curriculum for English at Key Stage 1, Year 2 (England).

The *Pupil Books* provide children with a reminder of **the spelling rule** for the session and a collection of **activities** to consolidate learning. Some activities highlight the meanings of the words in the Word Bank, while others remind children to pay careful attention to the letters within those words.

Activities can be completed as a **whole class**, or as **independent work**.

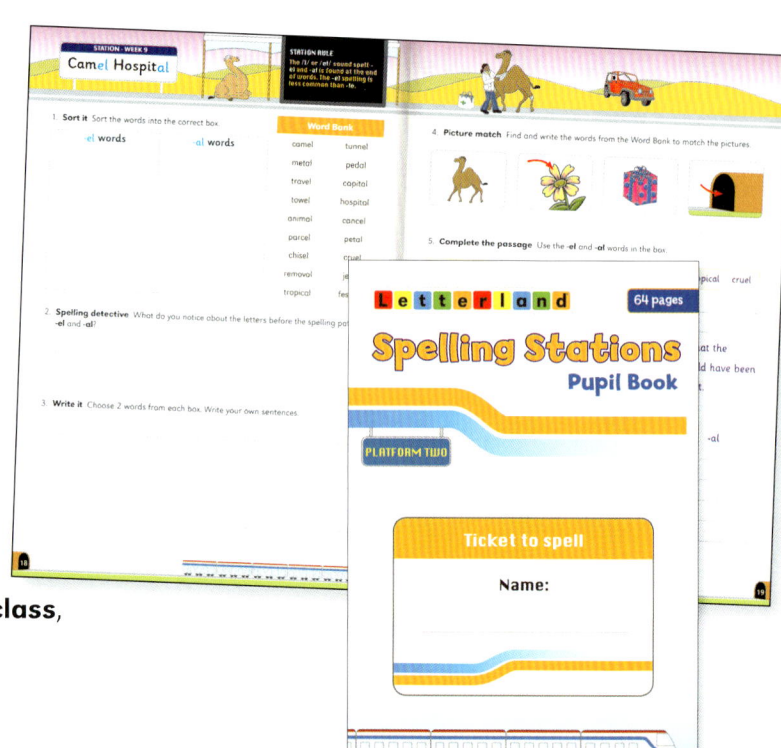

Spelling Stations Ticket Book - Platform Two

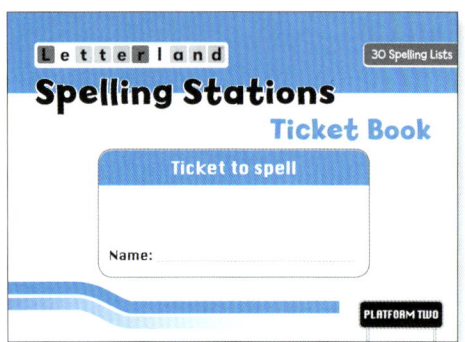

Each child should have a copy of the *Spelling Stations Ticket Book*. The book contains all the Word Banks and spelling patterns they will learn throughout the year. It provides a collection of spelling knowledge to be kept and referred to as needed.

Each week children will be tested on the words from **one ticket**. Children will have covered the spelling patterns in class, and they should also be encouraged to revise the spellings in the *Spelling Stations Ticket Book* at home with a parent/carer.

The tickets provide a record of how each child is progressing with their spelling. Getting a ticket stamped each week by the teacher gives a real sense of accomplishment.

When all the tickets are stamped, your pupils will be ready to move forward on their spelling journeys!

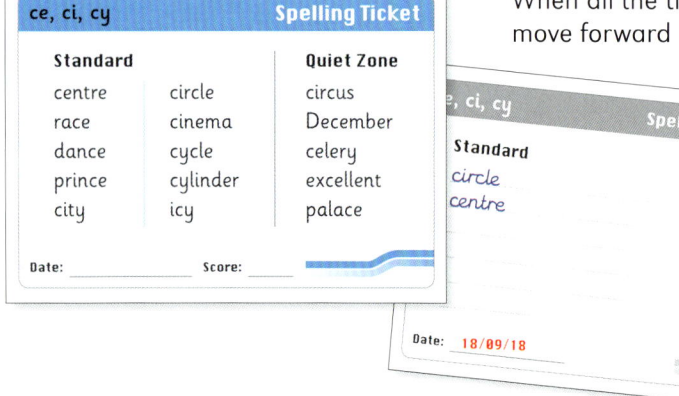

Ticket Book - Word Bank

Standard: 10-12 words per week	Quiet Zone: 3-6 words per week
Words that exemplify applicable syllable or spelling patterns as outlined in the curriculum* Common exception 'tricky' words	Words of interest that spur further engagement with vocabulary for those children who need more of a challenge

*National Curriculum for England

Week	Focus	Standard	Quiet Zone
1	Year 1 Review	puffin, doll, press, buzz, duck, skip, give, catch, hats, foxes, happy, sink, carrot, jumping, farmer, rested, shorter, fastest, rain, play, gate, theme, bike, hope, June, sheep, leaf, star	
2	Year 1 Review	person, winter, girl, Thursday, food, book, road, toe, snow, friend, mouth, crown, blue, news, Tuesday, lie, light, boy, coin, fork, August, draw, air, care, pear, dolphin, white, unlock	
3	ge dge	age, huge, change, page, large, stage badge, edge, bridge, fridge, hedge, judge	village, package, damage trudge, porridge, smudge
4	ge gi gy	gem, gentle, germ, danger giant, ginger, magic energy, gymnast, allergy	vegetable engine, giraffe, register apology
5	ce ci cy	centre, race, dance, prince city, circle, cinema cycle, cylinder, icy	circus, December, celery, excellent, palace
6	kn gn	knock, know, knee, knife, knight gnat, gnaw, gnome, sign, design	knit, kneel, knot gnarled, gnash
7	wr	write, wrote, written, wrong, wrist, wrap, wrapper, wrinkle, wreck, wriggle	wrench, wrestle, wrath, wrung
8	le	table, apple, bottle, little, middle, jungle, needle, scribble, stable, puddle	purple, bubble, cable, beetle, kettle
9	el al	camel, tunnel, travel, towel, cancel, parcel metal, pedal, capital, hospital, animal, petal	cruel, jewel removal, tropical, festival
10	il	pencil, fossil, nostril, gerbil, basil, evil, pupil, April, stencil, utensil	civil, lentil
11	y /igh/	cry, fly, dry, try, reply, July, shy, sky, spy, my, by, sty	fry, buy, guy, why, multiply, simplify
12	–y to –ies	lorries, ladies, babies, berries, pennies, worries flies, cries, tries, replies, dries, bunnies	hobbies, cities, copies, jellies
13	–ing –ed –er –est	crying, carried, happier, hurried, copying, funniest, emptying, sillier, busiest, copied, lazier, laziest	studying, supplied, luckiest, replied, chillier, prettier
14	–ing –ed –er –est –y	bravest, exciting, closer, invited, wiped, stripy, largest, sneezed, nicer, sliding, wisest, shiny	fiercest, gentler, moving, juicy, noisy, arrived

Week	Focus	Standard	Quiet Zone
15	–ing –ed –er –est –y	patting, runny, sadder, funny, dropping, bigger, muddy, daddy, slipping, mummy, skipping, hotter	hummed, thinnest, hopped, stopped, fatter, chatted
16	Tricky Words	door, floor, poor, find, kind, mind, behind, child, wild, most, only, both, old, cold, gold, hold, told, every, everybody, even, plant	pretty, climb, great, break, steak, because, children
17	all al /or/	small, stall, stalk, ball, call, walk, tall, always, fall, talk	smallest, calling, walked, taller
18	o /u/	honey, glove, love, son, mother, brother, other, nothing, Monday, oven	dozen, another, cover, above
19	ey /ee/	donkey, valley, monkey, money, key, chimney, turkey, hockey, jockey, trolley	journey, alley, kidney, pulley
20	qua /o/ wa /o/	quantity, squash, squat, qualified, quality watch, want, wasp, swan, wash	quarrel, swallow wander, wallet, swamp,
21	war /or/ wor /er/	warm, warn, swarm, reward, towards world, word, worm, work, worst	wardrobe, war dwarf, worth
22	s /zh/	measure, pleasure, treasure, television, usual, discussion, division, confusion, extension, explosion, conclusion, invasion	possession, expression, revision, progression, collusion, occasion
23	–ly –ment	badly, happily, slowly, quickly, softly, loudly, lovely, refreshment, enjoyment, payment, movement, pavement	safely, lonely, excitement, agreement, amazement
24	–ful –less –ness	careful, playful, helpful, tearful, careless, useless, fearless, hopeless sadness, darkness, fairness, kindness	forgetful, cheerful effortless, thoughtless plainness, foolishness
25	Contractions	don't, can't, won't, I've, wasn't, he'd, she'd, they'd, they've, they're, we're, we've	hasn't, couldn't, shouldn't wouldn't, haven't, didn't
26	Possessive apostrophes	Tom's, Kate's, Ravi's, boy's, girl's, cat's, dog's, man's, shop's, baby's	woman's, doctor's, teacher's, tree's, Tess's
27	–tion	action, station, mention, fiction, motion, section, fraction, lotion, education, pollution, relation, competition	explanation, completion, imagination, operation, introduction
28	Homophones and near homophones	blue/blew, sea/see, here/hear, bare/bear, one/won, sun/son, to/too/two, be/bee, night/knight	there/they're/their quite/quiet
29	Tricky Words	busy, people, after, fast, last, past, father, class, grass, pass, plant, path, bath, hour, move, prove, improve, eye, could, should, would, who, clothes, money, parents	sure, sugar, water, many, any, again, half, Mr, Mrs, Christmas
30	Year 1 and 2 Review	miss, think, rocket, catch, have, cats, jumping, fresher, rain, day, made, these, five, home, rule, car, tree, dream, bread, person, summer, bird, turn, moon, book, boat, toes, mouth, brown, snow, blue, grew, pie, field, light, horse, yawn, hair, beard, pear, care, happy, dolphin, wheel, skin, unlock, football, bridge, giraffe, race, circle, knee, gnome, write, table, animal, pencil, cry, babies, walk, brother, key, word, warm, treasure, didn't, Tim's, station, helpful, badly, watched, fastest	

STATION - WEEK 1
Ready to Depart
PLATFORM ONE REVIEW

OBJECTIVES
Spell and use words in writing containing spelling patterns learnt in Year One

Introducing Letterland Spelling

As this is the start of *Letterland Spelling Stations - Platform Two,* the first two lessons will review content from *Spelling Stations - Platform One*. This is a revision of the statutory requirements for Spelling in the National Curriculum for English at Key Stage 1, Year 1 (England), and does not require or rely upon students having used *Spelling Stations - Platform One* in order to complete these review lessons.

Ask the children to think about whether they always spell words with the correct letters. Elicit ideas and remind the children that spelling in English is very difficult because we have multiple ways of writing some sounds, for example there are different ways to spell the /j/ sound (**j**, **-ge**, **-dge**, **ge**, **gi**, **gy**). Reassure the children that over time they will learn how to spell correctly using the *Letterland Spelling Stations* and that it will be great fun!

Introducing the rule

Each lesson has a rule. Within this guide we use the terms **consonants** and **long and short vowels**. It is important that children understand these terms so check this at the very start of your first lesson. Some children find describing sounds as 'long' or 'short' as quite a difficult concept. They benefit from having a visual prompt with ideational content which can then become their recall route if they forget which is which. *Letterland Phonics* (see pages 112-115) provides child-friendly characters and stories to associate with vowels to prevent any confusion. Explain to the children that in today's lesson they will revise words that contain spelling patterns from *Spelling Stations - Platform One*.

Each child should be given their own *Spelling Stations Pupil Book - Platform Two*.

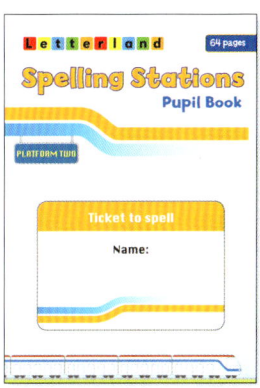

Pupil Book Activity 1: Solve the clues

1. Draw children's attention to the Word Bank at the top of page 2. Explain that all of these words contain spelling patterns that they learnt about in *Spelling Stations - Platform One*.
2. Ask the children to read through the words in the Word Bank and talk to a partner about what they mean. Then ask the children if there are any words they are unsure of and explain the meanings to them, looking in the dictionary for a definition if necessary.
3. Ask the children to read each clue, then find the answer words in the Word Bank and write them in the spaces provided.

Answers: a) duck; b) carrot; c) star; d) farmer; e) bike; f) June

Pupil Book Activity 2: Write it

1. Model the activity by showing the children how to think of, say and write a sentence using the first word, press. Write your sentence on the board to show correct punctuation and handwriting. For example, say: What does press mean? Press a button or a switch. So my sentence could be 'Press the switch to turn on the light'.
2. Ask the children to write a sentence for each of the given words. If children need support they could work in pairs to decide on a sentence and say it outloud before writing it. If children need further support use these example answers to provide a dictated sentence (the adult reads the sentence and the children write it).

Example answers:

a) press: Press the switch to turn on the light.

b) jumping: We were jumping on the trampoline.

c) today: Today is Monday.

d) rain: I walked to school in the rain.

e) fastest: Tom is the fastest runner in our class.

Pupil Book Activity 3: Write a story

1. Set the children the challenge of writing their own short story using the items in the picture. Explain to the children that using the words in this way will help them to remember the words more effectively. Encourage the children to include as many of the other Word Bank words as possible.

2. Use the following text as a model to show the children how to write the short story or, alternatively, use the text as a passage dictation by reading each sentence slowly and clearly for the children to write down:

James went on a train journey with his mum. They saw some puffins on the cliff. Then they saw a farmer herding some sheep in a field. When the train stopped, James and his mum put on their hats because it was cold outside. As they stepped off the train, James saw a doll that had been left behind on the train seat.

Pupil Book Activity 4: Pair work

1. Ask the children to look at each word in the table. Tell them to read the words themselves first. Then ask the children to work in pairs. One partner reads the words aloud, while the other writes them down on a separate piece of paper without looking in their book. Swap over roles.

2. When they have finished, the children can open their books and mark their own answers by colouring the boxes. They use green if they have spelt the word correctly, orange if they think they know the spelling but made a small error or red if they feel they struggle with the spelling of the word.

3. Ask children to think about whether they find each word easy to spell, difficult to spell or somewhere inbetween.

Note: This is a valuable activity to encourage the children to be reflective and develop an awareness of words that are easier and harder for them. Children's responses also provide an informative indication for adults of how they feel about spelling. Perhaps they colour lots of words with red when they can, in fact, spell many of them. This might show that they still feel as if spelling is difficult, which is preventing them from seeing their own progress.

Assessment

Hand out a copy of the *Spelling Stations Ticket Book - Platform Two* to each child.

Explain that this is their book of tickets and, as with any ticket, it is very important that it isn't lost or damaged. Each week they will need to learn the spellings on **one ticket**. They can write the date on the ticket they need to learn (or you can date stamp it).

Encourage children to learn their weekly spelling ticket at home. There are strategies at the beginning of the *Ticket Book* to help guide parents/carers.

Full details of how to carry out assessment can be found on pages 6 and 102 of this guide.

Assessment: Review Platform One

Most children should be able to successfully participate in a rapid pace word assessment, which will enable you to quickly take a baseline score of their current spelling ability. To do this, tell the children that you are going to call out lots of words, one at a time. Each word will be one of the review words that they have been practising. Tell the children that you will say the word then repeat it as they write it down.

1. puffin
2. duck
3. hats
4. carrot
5. shorter
6. rain
7. bike
8. leaf
9. doll
10. skip
11. foxes
12. jumping
13. play
14. hope
15. press
16. give
17. happy
18. farmer
19. gate
20. June
21. buzz
22. catch
23. sink
24. rested
25. fastest
26. theme
27. sheep
28. star

If you have children in your class that may not be ready for the rapid word test, you can still test the words but in four smaller sessions, perhaps one session per day across four days. Tell the children that you are going to read out seven words, one at a time. Each word will be one of the *Spelling Station - Platform One* words that they have been reviewing. Tell the children that you will say the word, and then you will read out a sentence containing the word to help them remember what it means. You will then repeat the word on its own again before pausing so that the children can write the word down. For example: 1. **puffin**. We saw a **puffin** on the cliff. **puffin**

Test 1

1. **puffin**. We saw a **puffin** on the cliff. **puffin**
2. **duck**. The **duck** swims on the pond. **duck**
3. **hats**. I have **hats** for hot and cold days. **hats**
4. **carrot**. My rabbit ate a **carrot** for dinner. **carrot**
5. **shorter**. I am **shorter** than my brother. **shorter**
6. **rain**. I wear boots in the **rain**. **rain**
7. **bike**. I can ride my **bike**. **bike**

Test 2

1. **leaf**. The **leaf** fell from the tree. **leaf**
2. **doll**. We gave Poppy a new **doll**. **doll**
3. **skip**. I **skip** along the path. **skip**
4. **foxes**. The **foxes** sleep in the day. **foxes**
5. **jumping**. I was **jumping** up and down. **jumping**
6. **play**. My sister likes to **play** football. **play**
7. **hope**. I **hope** we will visit Gran soon. **hope**

Test 3

1. **press**. **Press** the button to turn on the torch. **press**
2. **give**. I will **give** this letter to my mum. **give**
3. **happy**. I am always **happy** in the mornings. **happy**
4. **farmer**. My dad is a **farmer**. **farmer**
5. **gate**. Mum forgot to shut the garden **gate**. **gate**
6. **June**. My birthday is in **June**. **June**
7. **sink**. We wash our hands in the **sink**. **sink**

Test 4

1. **buzz**. I heard the **buzz** of a bumblebee. **buzz**
2. **catch**. I can **catch** the ball. **catch**
3. **rested**. I have **rested** my sore foot. **rested**
4. **fastest**. Tom is the **fastest** runner. **fastest**
5. **theme**. My party has a mermaid **theme**. **theme**
6. **sheep**. We saw a large flock of **sheep**. **sheep**
7. **star**. Our sun is a huge **star**. **star**.

STATION - WEEK 2

On Track
PLATFORM ONE REVIEW

OBJECTIVES
Spell and use words in writing containing spelling patterns learnt in Year One

Review previous learning

Ask the children if they can recall the spelling content and any examples from the previous spelling lesson. Elicit ideas and remind the children that they were revising words from *Spelling Stations - Platform One*, for example: **buzz**, **fastest**, **jumping**.

Introducing the rule

Explain to the children that in today's lesson they will continue to revise more words that contain spelling patterns from *Spelling Stations - Platform One*.

Pupil Book Activity 1: Solve the clues

1. Draw children's attention to the Word Bank at the top of page 4. Explain that all of these words contain spelling patterns that they learnt about in *Spelling Stations - Platform One*.
2. Ask the children to read through the words in the Word Bank and talk to a partner about what they mean. Then ask the children if there are any words they are unsure of and explain the meanings to them, looking in the dictionary for a definition if necessary.
3. Ask the children to read each clue, then find the answer words in the Word Bank and write them in the spaces provided.

Answers: a) crown; b) coin; c) pear; d) snow; e) book; f) August

Pupil Book Activity 2: Write it

1. Model the activity by showing the children how to think of, say and write a sentence using the first word, friend. Write your sentence on the board to show correct punctuation and handwriting. For example, say: What does a friend do? Play games with other friends. So my sentence could be 'I play football with my friend'.
2. Ask the children to write a sentence for each of the given words. If children need support they could work in pairs to decide on a sentence and say it aloud before writing it. If children need further support use these example answers to provide a dictated sentence (the adult reads the sentence and the children write it).

Example answers:

a) friend: I play football with my friend.

b) dolphin: The dolphin swam in the sea.

c) girl: The girl brushed her hair.

d) unlock: We use the key to unlock the door.

e) draw: I like to draw cars.

Pupil Book Activity 3: Write a story

1. Set the children the challenge of writing their own short story using the items in the picture. Explain to the children that using the words in this way will help them to remember the words more effectively. Encourage the children to include as many of the other Word Bank words as possible.
2. Use the following text as a model to show the children how to write the short story or, alternatively, use the text as a passage dictation by reading each sentence slowly and clearly for the children to write down:

Fay watched the man eat a pear and read his newspaper on the train. The news story on the cover was about a boy who had discovered an old fork under the ground in his garden. He had stubbed his toe on the end which was sticking up. The fork was very old and had marks carved into it.

Pupil Book Activity 4: Pair work

1. Ask the children to look at each word in the table. Tell them to read the words themselves first. Then ask the children to work in pairs. One partner reads the words aloud, while the other writes them down on a separate piece of paper without looking in their book. Swap over roles.

2. When they have finished, the children can open their books and mark their own answers by colouring the boxes. They use green if they have spelt the word correctly, orange if they think they know the spelling but made a small error or red if they feel they struggle with the spelling of the word.

3. Ask children to think about whether they find each word easy to spell, difficult to spell or somewhere inbetween.

Note: This is a valuable activity to encourage the children to be reflective and develop an awareness of words that are easier and harder for them. Children's responses also provide an informative indication for adults of how they feel about spelling. Perhaps they colour lots of words with red when they can, in fact, spell many of them. This might show that they still feel as if spelling is difficult, which is preventing them from seeing their own progress.

Assessment: Review Platform One

Most children should be able to successfully participate in a rapid pace word assessment, which will enable you to quickly take a baseline score of their current spelling ability. To do this, tell the children that you are going to call out lots of words, one at a time. Each word will be one of the review words that they have been practising. Tell the children that you will say the word then repeat it as they write it down.

1. person
2. food
3. snow
4. crown
5. Tuesday
6. coin
7. draw
8. pear
9. winter
10. book
11. blue
12. lie
13. fork
14. air
15. dolphin
16. girl
17. road
18. friend
19. light
20. white
21. Thursday
22. toe
23. mouth
24. news
25. boy
26. August
27. care
28. unlock

If you have children in your class that may not be ready for the rapid word test, you can still test the words but in four smaller sessions, perhaps one session per day across four days. Tell the children that you are going to read out seven words, one at a time. Each word will be one of the *Spelling Stations - Platform One* words that they have been reviewing. Tell the children that you will say the word, and then you will read out a sentence containing the word to help them remember what it means. You will then repeat the word on its own again before pausing so that the children can write the word down. For example: 1. **person**. My teacher is a kind **person**. **person**

Test 1

1. **person**. My teacher is a kind **person**. **person**
2. **food**. We shop for **food** at the market. **food**
3. **snow**. I dress up warmly to play in the **snow**. **snow**
4. **crown**. If I were a king, I would wear a **crown**. **crown**
5. **Tuesday**. Monday comes before **Tuesday**. **Tuesday**
6. **coin**. I found a shiny silver **coin**. **coin**

7. **draw**. I like to **draw** trees. **draw**

Test 2

1. **winter**. After **winter** comes spring. **winter**
2. **book**. I have finished reading my **book**. **book**
3. **blue**. My new trainers are **blue**. **blue**
4. **lie**. I try to never tell a **lie**. **lie**
5. **fork**. I ate my pasta with a knife and **fork**. **fork**
6. **air**. The hairdryer blasts out hot **air**. **air**
7. **unlock**. We twisted the key to **unlock** the door. **unlock**

Test 3

1. **dolphin**. The **dolphin** swam in the sea. **dolphin**
2. **girl**. The **girl** brushed her hair. **girl**
3. **road**. We drove down the **road**. **road**
4. **friend**. My **friend** invited me to a party. **friend**
5. **light**. Mum turned off the **light**. **light**
6. **care**. I take **care** of our baby rabbits. **care**
7. **pear**. I have a **pear** in my lunchbox. **pear**

Test 4

1. **white**. The clouds are **white** and fluffy today. **white**
2. **Thursday**. I am going swimming on **Thursday**. **Thursday**
3. **toe**. I bumped my big **toe**. **toe**
4. **mouth**. I opened my **mouth** to yawn. **mouth**
5. **news**. Tom told me the **news**. **news**
6. **boy**. A new **boy** joined our class. **boy**
7. **August**. In **August** we are going on holiday. **August**

MIND THE GAP!

After reviewing the children's Platform One Assessments (conducted during weeks 1 and 2), you may decide to use the information to influence the teaching of spelling moving forwards.

The target score for spelling is 80%. This means that children who achieve a score of 80% in the Platform One Assessments are ready to progress onto *Spelling Stations Platform Two,* week 3 onwards.

Children that score less than 80% in the Platform One Assessments may need additional spelling support. This could take several forms. Depending on the number of children in the class that score below 80%, and those that score below 50%, you may wish to teach spelling as a whole class activity but with intervention group support, or alternatively you may wish to split the class into up to three differentiated groups.

Children that are working below age-related expectations can be supported in the following ways:

- Pinpoint where the 'gaps' are by analysing the children's answers to the Platform One Assessments, then use *Spelling Stations - Platform One* content to revise identified spelling patterns.
- Revisit targeted areas using *Letterland Phonics Teacher's Guide* or *Letterland Grammar Teacher's Guide.*
- Increase the use of mnemonic systems such as the Letterland Stories and characters to focus on supporting children's ability to remember and recall.
- Reduce the number of spellings expected per week.

It is important to remember that whilst children working below age-related expectations should be supported by revisiting and consolidating previous spellings that are still insecure, they should not be withheld from exposure to new, age-appropriate spellings.

Children that score 80%+ in the Platform One Assessments should be considered for the additional 'Quiet Zone' words.

Step-by-Step
Lesson Plans – Platform Two

STATION - WEEK 3

Huge Bridge

OBJECTIVES

ge and **dge**

Spell and use words containing **ge** or **dge**

Review previous learning

Ask the children if they can recall the spelling content and any examples from the previous spelling lesson. Elicit ideas and remind the children that they were revising words from *Spelling Stations - Platform One*, for example: **dolphin**, **news**, **boy**.

Introducing the rule

Explain to the children that in today's lesson they will learn about words that are spelt with **ge** and **dge** for the /j/ sound.

At the end of a word, the /j/ sound is spelt –**dge** after the /a/, /e/, /i/, /o/, /u/ sounds ('short' vowels), for example, **bridge**.

After all other sounds, whether vowels or consonants, the /j/ sound is spelt –**ge** at the end of a word, for example, **page**.

> **Optional: Review the Letterland character stories**
>
> Learning about Gentle Ginger the Gymnast may help children to remember this spelling pattern (see page 114).

Pupil Book Activity 1: Sort it

1. Draw children's attention to the Word Bank at the top of page 6. Explain that all of these words contain either the spelling pattern **ge** or **dge** for the /j/ sound.
2. Ask the children to read through the words in the Word Bank and talk to a partner about what they mean. Then ask the children if there are any words they are unsure of and explain the meanings to them, looking in the dictionary for a definition if necessary.
3. Ask the children to sort and write each word into the correct box according to the spelling pattern it contains.

ge	dge
page	bridge
package	hedge
damage	fridge
village	edge
huge	badge
change	porridge
age	judge
large	trudge
stage	smudge

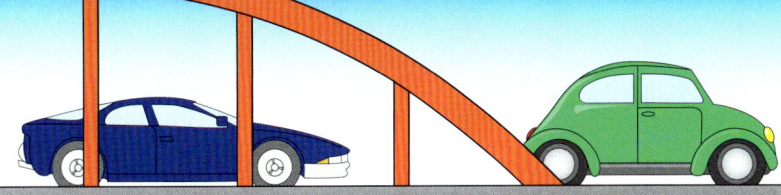

Pupil Book Activity 2: Spelling detective

1. Ask the children to tell you what they notice about the vowel sounds before the spelling patterns **ge** and **dge**. To support them, you could ask them to find and underline the vowel sound before the spelling patterns.
2. Some children may struggle to understand the significance until you demonstrate by saying the vowel sound aloud to show the difference between the short and long sounds.
3. Support the children to put their findings into a sentence, for example: A short vowel sound comes before –**dge** and a long vowel sound comes before –**ge**.

Pupil Book Activity 3: Write it

1. Model the activity by showing the children how to think of, say and write a sentence using a word from one of the word boxes in Activity 1, for example, **bridge**. Write your sentence on the board to show correct punctuation and handwriting formation. For example, say: What is a bridge? It goes over something like a river. So my sentence could be 'We drove across the bridge and looked at the water below'.
2. Ask the children to write a sentence for two words chosen from each box. If children need some support, they could work in pairs to decide on the words, then create a sentence and say it outloud before writing it. If children need full support, use these example answers to provide a dictated sentence (the adult reads the sentence and the children write it).

Example answers:

a) page: I turned the page in my book.

b) package: The postman delivered the package.

c) village: We moved house to a village.

d) hedge: I saw a bird's nest in the hedge.

e) porridge: I like eating porridge for breakfast.

Pupil Book Activity 4: Picture match

Remind the children of the Word Bank at the top of page 6.

1. Ask the children to find and copy words from the Word Bank to match the pictures.

Answers: a) bridge; b) fridge; c) porridge; d) package

Pupil Book Activity 5: Complete the passage

1. Read the passage to the children, pausing as you reach each gap. Complete the first gap with the children by re-reading to that point and then say: Look at the Word Bank. Which word is something that you might deliver to somebody? Elicit children's ideas and establish that the word is **package**.
2. Ask the children to fill in the gaps in the rest of the passage independently or with a partner.

Answers: David got off the train at Huge Bridge station. He had a **package** to deliver to the lady that lived in the **village**. Her address was written on a **page** in his notebook but the ink was **smudged** so he couldn't read it. The box was a bit torn from the journey so he hoped it was not **damaged**. The path to the house was muddy so David **trudged** along slowly through it. When he finally reached the lady's house she greeted him with a warm bowl of **porridge**.

Pupil Book Activity 6: Word search

1. Draw the children's attention to the Word search at the bottom of page 7. Set the children the challenge of finding 6 **ge** and **dge** words in the word search. The words may be found horizontally from left to right or vertically from top to bottom.
2. Tell the children to circle each word as they find it and then write the words in the correct column.

Answers:

s	i	b	o	a	c
e	t	a	l	g	h
j	u	d	g	e	a
p	a	g	e	c	n
o	k	e	p	s	g
c	l	a	r	g	e

ge	dge
change	badge
large	judge
page	
age	

Additional teaching notes

An unusual spelling for the /j/ sound is **di** as in **soldier**.

Assessment: ge, dge

Tell the children that you are going to read out twelve words, one at a time. Each word will be one of the **ge** or **dge** words that they have been learning. Tell the children that you will say the word, and then you will read out a sentence containing the word to help them remember what it means. You will then repeat the word on its own again before pausing so that the children can write the word down.

For example: **age**. Your **age** is how old you are. **age**

1. **age**. Your **age** is how old you are. **age**
2. **edge**. I stood at the **edge** of the pool waiting to get in. **edge**
3. **change**. The shopkeeper handed me my **change**. **change**
4. **large**. My cat is **large** and fluffy. **large**
5. **badge**. I earned my recycling **badge**. **badge**
6. **stage**. We stood on the **stage** ready to sing. **stage**
7. **huge**. The new stone statue in the city is **huge**. **huge**
8. **bridge**. We drove across the **bridge**. **bridge**
9. **judge**. The **judge** said everything was fair. **judge**
10. **page**. I turned to a new **page** in my book. **page**
11. **hedge**. The hedgehog hid under the **hedge**. **hedge**
12. **fridge**. We keep food cold in the **fridge**. **fridge**

For those students who need a little more of a spelling challenge, read out the six further 'Quiet Zone' words to spell: **village, trudge, package, damage, smudge, porridge**.

Full details of how to carry out assessment can be found on pages 6 and 102 of this guide.

STATION - WEEK 4

Magic Gym

OBJECTIVES
ge, gi and **gy**
Spell and use words containing **ge, gi** or **gy**

Review previous learning

Ask the children if they can recall the spelling content and any examples from the previous spelling lesson. Elicit ideas and remind the children that: At the end of a word, the /j/ sound is spelt **–dge** after a short vowel sound, for example, bri**dge**. After all other sounds, whether vowel or consonants, the /j/ sound is spelt **–ge** at the end of a word, for example, hu**ge**.

Introducing the rule

Explain to the children that in today's lesson they will learn about words that are spelt with the spelling patterns **ge**, **gi** and **gy**. The sound /j/ is usually spelt with a letter **g** before the letters **e**, **i** and **y**, for example, **gem**, **giant** and **gym**. Sometimes people refer to this spelling as 'soft g'.

Optional: Review the Letterland character stories

Letterland character-based stories can help children to remember spelling patterns (see page 114).

Pupil Book Activity 1: Sort it

1. Draw children's attention to the Word Bank at the top of page 8. Explain that all of these words contain the spelling patterns **ge**, **gi** and **gy**.
2. Ask the children to read through the words in the Word Bank and talk to a partner about what they mean. Then ask the children if there are any words they are unsure of and explain the meanings to them, looking in the dictionary for a definition if necessary.
3. Ask the children to sort and write each word into the correct box according to the spelling pattern it contains.

Answers:

ge	gi	gy
gem	register	energy
danger	ginger	gymnast
germ	giant	apology
gentle	magic	allergy
angel	giraffe	
vegetable	engine	

Pupil Book Activity 2: Crossword

1. Model the activity by reading the first clue aloud twice and then look through the Word Bank to find the correct answer.
2. Ask the children to read each clue, then find the answer words in the Word Bank and write them in the spaces provided.

23

3. Then ask the children to copy their answers into the correct places on the crossword. Explain that this is a way of checking if they have solved the clues correctly. The answers should fit into the crossword.

Answers: a) giraffe; b) danger; c) gem; d) engine; e) giant

Pupil Book Activity 3: Choose a ditty

1. Ask the children to carefully read both ditties. Explain that when we want to remember how words are spelt, a useful method is to group them together into a fun ditty or phrase. When you think of one of the words in the ditty, you will automatically remember the other words that went with it.
2. The children could work independently or in pairs. Ask them to choose their favourite ditty and read it lots of times to try and learn it by heart. Challenge them to sing it to any simple melody.
3. Ask children to perform their ditty to the class by reciting or singing it.
4. As an extension to the task, you could also ask the children to find and underline the spelling patterns in the ditties, or draw a picture to illustrate one of them.

Ditties in this lesson:

Ginger the gerbil is a dangerous gymnast.

The magic giants fixed the engine using gems.

Pupil Book Activity 4: Picture match

1. Remind the children of the Word Bank at the top of page 8.
2. Ask the children to find and copy words from the Word Bank to match the pictures.

Answers: a) giraffe; b) danger; c) gem; d) gymnast

Pupil Book Activity 5: Anagrams

1. Draw the children's attention to the anagrams in Activity 5. Explain to the children that the words have been taken from the Word Bank and the letters have been jumbled up into the wrong order.
2. Ask them to look carefully at the jumbled letters and try to work out which words from the Word Bank they are, then correctly write them in the space provided. Remind the children of the spelling patterns as a clue to help them: the letter **g** will be followed by **e**, **i** or **y**.
3. As a method of self-checking, encourage the children to count how many letters are in the jumbled word and how many letters they have written in the correct spelling of the word to check that they are the same. If they aren't, suggest to the children that they check their spelling of the word.

Answers: a) germ; b) ginger; c) allergy; d) giant; e) gentle

Pupil Book Activity 6: Write a story

1. Set the children the challenge of writing their own short story using **ge**, **gi** and **gy** words chosen from the Word Bank. Explain to the children that using the words in this way will help them to remember the words more effectively. Encourage the children to include as many of the Word Bank words as possible.
2. Use the following text as a model to show the children how to write the short story or, alternatively, use the text as a passage dictation by reading each sentence slowly and clearly for the children to write down:

   Gemma was on her way to a magic show. She met a lady with a ginger cat. Gemma sneezed. She had an allergy to cats. When Gemma arrived at the Magic Show, she saw dangerous tricks and fantastic gymnasts.

Assessment: ge, gi, gy

Tell the children that you are going to read out ten words, one at a time. Each word will be one of the **ge**, **gi**, **gy** words that they have been learning. Tell the children that you will say the word, and then you will read out a sentence containing the word to help them remember what it means. You will then repeat the word on its own again before pausing so that the children can write the word down. For example: **gem**. The necklace had a sparkly **gem**. **gem**

1. **gem**. The necklace had a sparkly **gem**. **gem**
2. **germ**. A **germ** is like a bug that could make you ill. **germ**
3. **giant**. The **giant** lived at the top of the beanstalk. **giant**
4. **energy**. My little brother is full of **energy**. **energy**
5. **magic**. I saw a **magic** show at the party. **magic**
6. **ginger**. My nan put **ginger** in the cookie mix. **ginger**
7. **gymnast**. I am a good **gymnast**. **gymnast**
8. **allergy**. I have an **allergy** to nuts. **allergy**
9. **gentle**. We gave the kitten a **gentle** stroke. **gentle**
10. **danger**. Do not ignore a **danger** sign. **danger**.

For those students who need a little more of a spelling challenge, read out the further 'Quiet Zone' words to spell: **engine**, **register**, **allergy**, **giraffe, apology**

Full details of how to carry out assessment can be found on pages 6 and 102 of this guide.

STATION - WEEK 5

Ice City

OBJECTIVES
ce, ci and **cy**

Spell and use words containing **ce, ci** or **cy**

Review previous learning

Ask the children if they can recall the spelling content and any examples from the previous spelling lesson. Elicit ideas and remind the children that: The sound /j/ is usually spelt with a **g** before the letters **e**, **i** and **y**, for example, **gem**, **giant** and **gym**. Sometimes people refer to this spelling as 'soft g'.

Introducing the rule

Explain to the children that in today's lesson they will learn about words that are spelt with **c** for the /s/ sound when it comes before the letters **e**, **i** and **y**, for example **celery**, **circle** and **cycle**. Sometimes people refer to this spelling as 'soft c'.

> **Optional: Review the Letterland character stories**
> Letterland stories help children to remember these sounds (see page 114).

Pupil Book Activity 1: Sort it

1. Draw children's attention to the Word Bank at the top of page 10. Explain that all of these words contain the spelling patterns **ce**, **ci** and **cy**.
2. Ask the children to read through the words in the Word Bank and talk to a partner about what they mean. Then ask the children if there are any words they are unsure of and explain the meanings to them, looking in the dictionary for a definition if necessary.
3. Ask the children to sort and write each word into the correct box according to the spelling pattern it contains.

Answers:

ce		ci	cy
December	palace	cinema	fancy
race	France	city	icy
prince		circle	cycle
celery	excellent		cylinder
dance	centre	circus	cymbal

Pupil Book Activity 2: Write it

1. Model the activity by showing the children how to think of, say and write a sentence using a word from one of the word boxes in Activity 1, for example, **cinema**. Write your sentence on the board to show correct punctuation and handwriting formation. For example, say: What can you do at a cinema? Watch a film. So my sentence could be 'I went to the cinema to see a film'.
2. Ask the children to write a sentence for two words chosen from each box. If children need some support, they could work in pairs to decide on a sentence and say it outloud before writing it. If children need full support, use these example answers to provide a dictated sentence (the adult reads the sentence and the children write it).

Example answers:

a) December: My birthday is in December.

b) city: We went shopping in the city.

c) race: I took part in a big race at school.

d) icy: The path was icy in the morning.

e) circle: I drew a yellow circle.

Pupil Book Activity 3: Choose a ditty

1. Ask the children to carefully read both ditties. Explain that when we want to remember how words are spelt, a useful method is to group them together into a fun ditty or phrase. When you think of one of the words in the ditty, you will automatically remember the other words that went with it.
2. The children could work independently or in pairs. Ask them to choose their favourite ditty and read it lots of times to try and learn it by heart. Challenge them to sing it to any simple melody.
3. Ask children to perform their ditty to the class by reciting or singing it.
4. As an extension to the task, you could also ask the children to find and underline the spelling patterns in the ditties, or draw a picture to illustrate one of them.

Ditties in this lesson:

The excellent cycle race was held in the city in France.

There is an excellent fancy palace in the icy city.

Pupil Book Activity 4: Picture match

1. Remind the children of the Word Bank at the top of page 10.
2. Ask the children to find and copy words from the Word Bank to match the pictures.

Answers: a) celery; b) palace; c) cycle; d) circle

Pupil Book Activity 5: Complete the passage

1. Read the passage to the children, pausing as you reach each gap. Complete the first gap with the children by re-reading to that point and then say: Look at the Word Bank. Which word is a month of the year? Elicit children's ideas and establish that the word is December.
2. Ask the children to fill in the gaps in the rest of the passage independently or with a partner.

Answers: Lucy's family arrived at the station for their big day out. The month was **December** and the streets were **icy**. The **city** was busy because everyone had come to see a new film at the **cinema.** It was about a big **cycle** **race** in **France**. Even a **prince** from the **palace** had come to see it!

Pupil Book Activity 6: Word search

1. Draw the children's attention to the word search at the bottom of page 11. Set the children the challenge of finding 6 **ce**, **ci** and **cy** words in the word search. The words may be found horizontally from left to right or vertically from top to bottom.
2. Tell the children to circle each word as they find it and then write the words in the correct column.

Answers:

c	d	a	n	c	e
i	c	i	t	y	g
n	a	d	i	h	c
e	r	a	c	e	d
m	c	y	c	l	e
a	i	c	y	a	b

ce	ci	cy
dance	cinema	cycle
race	city	icy

Assessment: ce, ci, cy

Tell the children that you are going to read out ten words, one at a time. Each word will be one of the **ce**, **ci** or **cy** words that they have been learning. Tell the children that you will say the word, and then you will read out a sentence containing the word to help them remember what it means. You will then repeat the word on its own again before pausing so that the children can write the word down.
For example: **centre**. I stood in the **centre** of the pitch. **centre**

1. **centre**. I stood in the **centre** of the pitch. **centre**
2. **city**. Mum got a new job in the **city**. **city**
3. **cycle**. I **cycle** to my nan's house on Saturdays. **cycle**
4. **race**. My friends had a **race** up the hill. **race**
5. **circle**. We sat in a **circle** shape. **circle**
6. **cinema**. My dad took us to the **cinema**. **cinema**
7. **cylinder**. The tin can was a **cylinder** shape. **cylinder**
8. **icy**. We nearly slipped on the **icy** road. **icy**
9. **dance**. I like to **dance** to pop music. **dance**
10. **prince**. The **prince** has a gold crown. **prince**

For those students who need a little more of a spelling challenge, read out the six further 'Quiet Zone' words to spell: **circus, December, celery, excellent, palace**

Full details of how to carry out assessment can be found on pages 6 and 102 of this guide.

STATION - WEEK 6

Knitted Gnomes

OBJECTIVES
kn and gn

Spell and use words containing **kn** or **gn**

Review previous learning

Ask the children if they can recall the spelling content and any examples from the previous spelling lesson. Elicit ideas and remind the children that: The /s/ sound is spelt as **c** before the letters **e**, **i** and **y**, for example **celery**, **circle**, **cycle**. Sometimes people refer to this spelling as 'soft c'.

Introducing the rule

Explain to the children that in today's lesson they will learn about words that are spelt with **kn** and **gn** for the /n/ sound. The /n/ sound is sometimes spelt **kn** and (less often) **gn** at the beginning of words, for example, **knit** and **gnome**.

Optional: Review the Letterland character stories

The Letterland stories help children to remember this spelling pattern (see page 114).

Pupil Book Activity 1: Sort it

1. Draw children's attention to the Word Bank at the top of page 12. Explain that all of these words contain the spelling patterns **kn** or **gn**.
2. Ask the children to read through the words in the Word Bank and talk to a partner about what they mean. Then ask the children if there are any words they are unsure of and explain the meanings to them, looking in the dictionary for a definition if necessary.
3. Ask the children to sort and write each word into the correct box according to the spelling pattern it contains.

Answers:

kn	gn
knock	gnat
knife	gnaw
knight	
knot	sign
know	
knee	gnome
kneel	design

Pupil Book Activity 2: Crossword

1. Model the activity by reading the first clue aloud twice and then look through the Word Bank to find the correct answer.
2. Ask the children to read each clue, then find the answer words in the Word Bank and write them in the spaces provided.

3. Then ask the children to copy their answers into the correct places on the crossword. Explain that this is a way of checking if they have solved the clues correctly. The answers should fit into the crossword.

Answers: a) knife; b) knee; c) gnome; d) knot; e) gnat

Pupil Book Activity 3: Choose a ditty

1. Ask the children to carefully read both ditties. Explain that when we want to remember how words are spelt, a useful method is to group them together into a fun ditty or phrase. When you think of one of the words in the ditty, you will automatically remember the other words that went with it.
2. The children could work independently or in pairs. Ask them to choose their favourite ditty and read it lots of times to try and learn it by heart. Challenge them to sing it to any simple melody.
3. Ask children to perform their ditty to the class by reciting or singing it.
4. As an extension to the task, you could also ask the children to find and underline the spelling patterns in the ditties, or draw a picture to illustrate one of them.

Ditties in this lesson:

The knight knew how to kneel but he wanted to know how to knit.

The gnome designed a sign to stop the gnat gnawing on things.

Pupil Book Activity 4: Picture match

1. Remind the children of the Word Bank at the top of page 12.
2. Ask the children to find and copy words from the Word Bank to match the pictures.

Answers: a) gnome; b) knot; c) knit; d) knight

Pupil Book Activity 5: Anagrams

1. Draw the children's attention to the anagrams in Activity 5. Explain to the children that the words have been taken from the Word Bank and the letters have been jumbled up into the wrong order.
2. Ask them to look carefully at the jumbled letters and try to work out which words from the Word Bank they are, then correctly write them in the space provided. Remind the children of the spelling patterns as a clue to help them: the letters **kn** and **gn** go together.
3. As a method of self-checking, encourage the children to count how many letters are in the jumbled word and how many letters they have written in the correct spelling of the word to check that they are the same. If they aren't, suggest to the children that they check their spelling of the word.

Answers: a) knock; b) gnome; c) sign; d) knight; e) design

Pupil Book Activity 6: Write a story

1. Set the children the challenge of writing their own short story using **kn** and **gn** words. Explain to the children that using the words in this way will help them to remember the words more effectively. Encourage the children to include as many of the Word Bank words as possible.
2. Use the following text as a model to show the children how to write the short story or, alternatively, use the text as a passage dictation by reading each sentence slowly and clearly for the children to write down:

Nelly was dressed up as a knight. Her Nan wanted to teach her how to knit. Nelly knew that she would end up in knots. Nelly's Nan had a new design for a tiny top. She wanted to knit a top for her garden gnome. Nelly smiled then carried on playing knights.

Did you know?

1. Tell the children that the 'k' and 'g' at the beginning of these words were sounded hundreds of years ago. Encourage them to say words from the Word Bank with the **k** and **g** pronounced.

Assessment: kn, gn

Tell the children that you are going to read out ten words, one at a time. Each word will be one of the **kn** or **gn** words that they have been learning. Tell the children that you will say the word, and then you will read out a sentence containing the word to help them remember what it means. You will then repeat the word on its own again before pausing so that the children can write the word down. For example: **knock**. I heard a **knock** on the door. **knock**

1. **knock**. I heard a **knock** on the door. **knock**
2. **know**. I **know** how excited you are. **know**
3. **gnat**. I saw a **gnat** fly past. **gnat**
4. **gnaw**. I watched the beaver **gnaw** the logs. **gnaw**
5. **knee**. I bumped my **knee** on the fence. **knee**
6. **gnome**. My nan has a new **gnome**. **gnome**
7. **knife**. You must take care with a **knife**. **knife**
8. **knight**. The **knight** rode his trusty steed. **knight**
9. **sign**. You must stop at a stop **sign**. **sign**
10. **design**. We could **design** a new garden. **design**

For those students who need a little more of a spelling challenge, read out the six further 'Quiet Zone' words to spell: **knit**, **kneel**, **knot**, **gnarled**, **gnash**.

Full details of how to carry out assessment can be found on pages 6 and 102 of this guide.

STATION - WEEK 7

Wrinkly Writer

OBJECTIVES
wr

Spell and use words containing **wr**

Review previous learning

Ask the children if they can recall the spelling content and any examples from the previous spelling lesson. Elicit ideas and remind the children that: The /n/ sound is sometimes spelt **kn** and (less often) **gn** at the beginning of words, for example, **knee** and **gnome**.

Introducing the rule

Explain to the children that in today's lesson they will learn about words that are spelt with **wr** for the /r/ sound at the beginning of the words, for example, **write** and **wrote**.

> **Optional: Review the Letterland character stories**
> The Letterland stories help children to remember this spelling pattern (see page 114).

Pupil Book Activity 1: Fill the gaps

1. Draw children's attention to the Word Bank at the top of page 14. Explain that all of these words contain the spelling pattern **wr** for the /r/ sound at the beginning of words.
2. Ask the children to read through the words in the Word Bank and talk to a partner about what they mean. Then ask the children if there are any words they are unsure of and explain the meanings to them, looking in the dictionary for a definition if necessary.
3. Ask the children to read each clue, then find the answer words in the Word Bank and write them in the spaces provided.

Answers: a) wrist; b) wreck; c) wrench; d) wrong; e) wrath

Pupil Book Activity 2: Write it

1. Model the activity by showing the children how to think of, say and write a sentence using a word from the Word Bank, for example, **write**. Write your sentence on the board to show correct punctuation and handwriting formation. For example, say: What does to **write** mean? Write words and sentences with a pencil. So my sentence could be 'I like to write long stories'.
2. Ask the children to write a sentence for 2 words chosen from the Word Bank. If children need some support, they could work in pairs to decide on a sentence and say it outloud before writing it. If children need full support, use these example answers to provide a dictated sentence (the adult reads the sentence and the children write it).

Example answers:

a) write: I like to write long stories.

b) wrong: If you get it wrong just try again.

c) wriggle: I watched a worm wriggle in the garden.

d) wrung: We wrung out the wet flannels.

e) wrapper: I peeled the wrapper off my snack bar.

Pupil Book Activity 3: Choose a ditty

1. Ask the children to carefully read both ditties. Explain that when we want to remember how words

are spelt, a useful method is to group them together into a fun ditty or phrase. When you think of one of the words in the ditty, you will automatically remember the other words that went with it.
2. The children could work independently or in pairs. Ask them to choose their favourite ditty and read it lots of times to try and learn it by heart. Challenge them to sing it to any simple melody.
3. Ask children to perform their ditty to the class by reciting or singing it.
4. As an extension to the task, you could also ask the children to find and underline the spelling patterns in the ditties, or draw a picture to illustrate one of them.

Ditties in this lesson:

We wrestled and wriggled to pull the wrinkled wrapper off the toy.

I wrote a note about my wrist but the note I wrote was wrong.

Pupil Book Activity 4: Picture match

1. Remind the children of the Word Bank at the top of page 14.
2. Ask the children to find and copy words from the Word Bank to match the pictures.

Answers: a) wrist; b) wrench; c) wreck; d) wrapper

Pupil Book Activity 5: Complete the passage

1. Read the passage to the children, pausing as you reach each gap. Complete the first gap with the children by re-reading to that point and then say: Look at the Word Bank. Which word is something that you might do to a new pen set? Elicit children's ideas and establish that the word is **unwrapped**.
2. Ask the children to fill in the gaps in the rest of the passage independently or with a partner.

Answers: Whilst on the train, Tom **unwrapped** his new pen set and **wrote** a story. It was about an old ship**wreck** under the sea. A sea monster was full of **wrath**. The monster **wrapped** its tentacles around the wreck. Tom loved to **write** stories but now his **wrist** hurt.

Pupil Book Activity 6: Word search

1. Draw the children's attention to the word search at the bottom of page 15. Set the children the challenge of finding 6 **wr** words in the word search. The words are all found horizontally from left to right.
2. Tell the children to circle each word as they find it and then write the words in the correct column.

Answers:

w	r	e	s	t	l	e
a	g	c	w	r	a	p
w	r	i	g	g	l	e
b	w	r	i	t	e	f
e	d	w	r	o	n	g
w	r	i	n	k	l	e

wr
wrestle
wrap
wriggle
write
wrong
wrinkle

Did you know?

1. Tell the children that the 'w' at the beginning of these words was sounded hundreds of years ago. Try saying the words in the Word Bank with the **w** pronounced.

Assessment: wr

Tell the children that you are going to read out ten words, one at a time. Each word will be one of the **wr** words that they have been learning. Tell the children that you will say the word, and then you will read out a sentence containing the word to help them remember what it means. You will then repeat the word on its own again before pausing so that the children can write the word down. For example: **write**. I like to **write** stories. **write**

1. **write**. I like to **write** stories. **write**
2. **wrote**. I **wrote** a thank you card to Nan. **wrote**
3. **written**. I have **written** out all of my spelling words. **written**
4. **wrong**. My dad is rarely **wrong** when spelling. **wrong**
5. **wrist**. Jane sprained her **wrist**. **wrist**
6. **wrap**. My sister ate a ham **wrap** for lunch. **wrap**
7. **wrapper**. I peeled the **wrapper** off the book. **wrapper**
8. **wrinkle**. I smoothed the **wrinkle** out of my bed sheets. **wrinkle**
9. **wreck**. The room looked like a **wreck**. **wreck**
10. **wriggle**. We watched the baby **wriggle** in her cot. **wriggle**

For those students who need a little more of a spelling challenge, read out the four further 'Quiet Zone' words to spell: **wrench**, **wrestle**, **wrath**, **wrung**.

Full details of how to carry out assessment can be found on pages 6 and 102 of this guide.

STATION - WEEK 8

Little Apples

OBJECTIVES
le

Spell and use words containing **le**

Review previous learning

Ask the children if they can recall the spelling content and any examples from the previous spelling lesson. Elicit ideas and remind the children that: The /r/ sound is sometimes spelt **wr** at the beginning of words, for example, **write** and **wrote**.

Introducing the rule

Explain to the children that in today's lesson they will learn about words that are spelt with **le** for the /l/ or /el/ sound at the end of words, for example, **table** and **apple**.

Optional: Review the Letterland character stories

The Letterland stories help children to remember this spelling pattern (see page 115).

Pupil Book Activity 1: Write it

1. Draw children's attention to the Word Bank at the top of page 16. Explain that all of these words contain the spelling pattern **le** for the /l/ or /el/ sound at the end of words.
2. Ask the children to read through the words in the Word Bank and talk to a partner about what they mean. Then ask the children if there are any words they are unsure of and explain the meanings to them, looking in the dictionary for a definition if necessary.
3. Model the activity by showing the children how to think of, say and write a sentence using the first word, **table**. Write your sentence on the board to show correct punctuation and handwriting formation. For example, say: What is a **table**? We eat our dinner at a **table**. So my sentence could be 'I put the plates on the table'.
4. Ask the children to write a sentence for each of the given words. If children need some support, they could work in pairs to decide on a sentence and say it outloud before writing it. If children need full support, use these example answers to provide a dictated sentence (the adult reads the sentence and the children write it).

Example answers:

a) scribble: My writing looked like a scribble.

b) little: I have a little sister.

c) middle: I live in the middle of the street.

d) puddle: The little girl jumped in the puddle.

Pupil Book Activity 2: Crossword

1. Model the activity by reading the first clue aloud twice and then look through the Word Bank to find the correct answer.
2. Ask the children to read each clue, then find the answer words in the Word Bank and write them in the spaces provided.
3. Then ask the children to copy their answers into the correct places on the crossword. Explain that this a way of checking if they have solved the clues correctly. The answers should fit into le crossword.

Answers: a) apple; b) needle; c) stable; d) jungle; e) beetle

Pupil Book Activity 3: Choose a ditty

1. Ask the children to carefully read both ditties. Explain that when we want to remember how words are spelt, a useful method is to group them together into a fun ditty or phrase. When you think of one of the words in the ditty, you will automatically remember the other words that went with it.
2. The children could work independently or in pairs. Ask them to choose their favourite ditty and read it lots of times to try and learn it by heart. Challenge them to sing it to any simple melody.
3. Ask children to perform their ditty to the class by reciting or singing it.
4. As an extension to the task, you could also ask the children to find and underline the spelling patterns in the ditties, or draw a picture to illustrate one of them.

Ditties in this lesson:

In the middle of a puddle in the jungle is a little purple beetle.

In the centre of the table is an apple, a bottle and a kettle.

Pupil Book Activity 4: Picture match

1. Remind the children of the Word Bank at the top of page 16.
2. Ask the children to find and copy words from the Word Bank to match the pictures.

Answers: a) apple; b) beetle; c) table; d) bottle

Pupil Book Activity 5: Anagrams

1. Draw the children's attention to the anagrams in Activity 5. Explain to the children that the words have been taken from the Word Bank and the letters have been jumbled up into the wrong order.
2. Ask them to look carefully at the jumbled letters and try to work out which words from the Word Bank they are, then correctly write them in the space provided. Remind the children of the spelling patterns as a clue to help them: the letters **l** and **e** go together for the /l/ sound at the end of words.
3. As a method of self-checking, encourage the children to count how many letters are in the jumbled word and how many letters they have written in the correct spelling of the word to check that they are the same. If they aren't, suggest to the children that they check their spelling of the word.

Answers: a) needle; b) scribble; c) stable; d) jungle; e) little

Pupil Book Activity 6: Write a story

4. Set the children the challenge of writing their own short story using **le** words. Explain to the children that using the words in this way will help them to remember the words more effectively. Encourage the children to include as many of the Word Bank words as possible.
5. Use the following text as a model to show the children how to write the short story or, alternatively, use the text as a passage dictation by reading each sentence slowly and clearly for the children to write down:

Outside the station was a large puddle. Jim saw a little beetle run around it, trying not to get wet. He checked that he had his water bottle, scribble pad and an apple in his backpack before he got on the train.

Did you know?

1. Tell the children that the **–le** spelling is the most common spelling for the /l/ sound at the end of words.
2. Other spelling patterns for the /l/ or /el/ sound at the end of words are **el**, **al** and **il**.

Assessment: le

Tell the children that you are going to read out ten words, one at a time. Each word will be one of the le words that they have been learning. Tell the children that you will say the word, and then you will read out a sentence containing the word to help them remember what it means. You will then repeat the word on its own again before pausing so that the children can write the word down. For example: **table**. I sat down at the **table**. **table**

1. **table**. I sat down at the **table**. **table**
2. **apple**. The best **apple** was the crunchy green one. **apple**
3. **bottle**. My water **bottle** is red. **bottle**
4. **little**. My **little** brother is cute. **little**
5. **middle**. We stood in the **middle** of the room. **middle**
6. **jungle**. My sister went on a trek in the **jungle**. **jungle**
7. **needle**. You need a **needle** to sew. **needle**
8. **scribble**. The toddler started to **scribble**. **scribble**
9. **stable**. The horses lived in the **stable**. **stable**
10. **puddle**. We jumped and splashed in the **puddle**. **puddle**

For those students who need a little more of a spelling challenge, read out the further 'Quiet Zone' words to spell: **purple**, **bubble**, **cable**, **beetle**, **kettle**

Full details of how to carry out assessment can be found on pages 6 and 102 of this guide.

STATION - WEEK 9

Camel Hospital

OBJECTIVES
el and al

Spell and use words containing el or al

Review previous learning

Ask the children if they can recall the spelling content and any examples from the previous spelling lesson. Elicit ideas and remind the children that: The /l/ or /el/ sound is most commonly spelt as **le** at the end of words, for example, **table** and **apple**.

Introducing the rule

Explain to the children that in today's lesson they will learn about words that are spelt with **–el** and **–al** for the /l/ or /el/ sound at the end of words. The /l/ or /el/ sound spelt **–el** and **–al** is often found at the end of words. The **–el** spelling is much less common than **–le**. The **–el** spelling is used after the letters **m**, **n**, **r**, **s**, **v**, **w** and more often than not, after the **s** sound.

> **Optional: Review the Letterland character stories**
> The Letterland stories help children to remember this spelling pattern (see page 115).

Pupil Book Activity 1: Sort it

1. Draw children's attention to the Word Bank at the top of page 18. Explain that all of these words contain the spelling patterns **–el** and **–al** for the /l/ or /el/ sound at the end of words.
2. Ask the children to read through the words in the Word Bank and talk to a partner about what they mean. Then ask the children if there are any words they are unsure of and explain the meanings to them, looking in the dictionary for a definition if necessary.
3. Ask the children to sort and write each word into the correct box according to the spelling pattern it contains.

Answers:

el	al
camel	metal
tunnel	pedal
travel	capital
towel	hospital
cancel	animal
parcel	petal
chisel	removal
cruel	tropical
jewel	festival

Pupil Book Activity 2: Spelling detective

1. Ask the children to tell you what they notice about the letters before the spelling patterns **el** and **al**. To support them, you could ask them to find and underline the letter before the spelling patterns.

2. Support the children to put their findings into a sentence, for example: The spelling pattern **el** comes after the letters **m**, **n**, **v**, **w**, **c** (as a /s/ sound), **s** and **u**. The spelling pattern **al** comes after the letters **t**, **d**, **m**, **v** and **c**.

Pupil Book Activity 3: Write it

1. Model the activity by showing the children how to think of, say and write a sentence using a word from one of the word boxes in Activity 1, for example, **camel**. Write your sentence on the board to show correct punctuation and handwriting formation. For example, say: What is a **camel**? It is an animal that lives in the desert. So my sentence could be 'The camel plodded through the desert'.
2. Ask the children to write a sentence for two words chosen from each box. If children need some support, they could work in pairs to decide on the words, then create a sentence and say it outloud before writing it. If children need full support, use these example answers to provide a dictated sentence (the adult reads the sentence and the children write it).

Example answers:

a) tunnel: The train travelled through the tunnel.

b) metal: The shed was made from metal.

c) towel: I packed my towel for swimming.

d) hospital: We had an appointment at the hospital.

Pupil Book Activity 4: Picture match

1. Remind the children of the Word Bank at the top of page 18.
2. Ask the children to find and copy words from the Word Bank to match the pictures.

Answers: a) camel; b) petal; c) parcel; d) tunnel

Pupil Book Activity 5: Complete the passage

1. Read the passage to the children, pausing as you reach each gap. Complete the first gap with the children by re-reading to that point and then say: Look at the Word Bank. Which word is something that a train can go through? Elicit children's ideas and establish that the word is **tunnel**.
2. Ask the children to fill in the gaps in the rest of the passage independently or with a partner.

Answers: The train went through the **tunnel** and past the **hospital**. At the station, Becky saw a big sign about an **animal** **festival** that was **cancelled**. The sign said that the **camels** had a **tropical** flu virus and it would have been **cruel** to let people visit them when they needed rest.

Pupil Book Activity 6: Word search

1. Draw the children's attention to the word search at the bottom of page 19. Set the children the challenge of finding 6 **el** and **al** words in the word search. The words may be found horizontally from left to right or vertically from top to bottom.
2. Tell the children to circle each word as they find it and then write the words in the correct column.

m	e	t	a	l	c
c	a	n	c	e	l
t	r	a	v	e	l
a	p	e	t	a	l
a	p	e	d	a	l
t	o	w	e	l	b

el	al
cancel	metal
travel	petal
towel	pedal

Did you know?

Tell the children that not many nouns end in –**al**, but many adjectives do.

Assessment: el, al

Tell the children that you are going to read out twelve words, one at a time. Each word will be one of the **el** or **al** words that they have been learning. Tell the children that you will say the word, and then you will read out a sentence containing the word to help them remember what it means. You will then repeat the word on its own again before pausing so that the children can write the word down. For example: **camel**. The **camel** plodded through the desert. **camel**

1. **camel**. The **camel** plodded through the desert. **camel**
2. **cancel**. Bad weather meant we had to **cancel** the trip. **cancel**
3. **metal**. You can recycle some types of **metal**. **metal**
4. **animal**. We went to visit an **animal** park. **animal**
5. **tunnel**. We ran through the **tunnel**. **tunnel**
6. **parcel**. The postman delivered the **parcel**. **parcel**
7. **pedal**. Dad fixed my bike **pedal**. **pedal**
8. **petal**. I carefully drew the flower **petal**. **petal**
9. **travel**. We love to **travel** on boats. **travel**
10. **capital**. I wrote my name in **capital** letters. **capital**
11. **towel**. After swimming, I dried myself with a **towel**. **towel**
12. **hospital**. The ambulance arrived at the **hospital**. **hospital**

For those students who need a little more of a spelling challenge, read out the further 'Quiet Zone' words to spell: **cruel**, **jewel**, **removal**, **tropical**, **festival**

Full details of how to carry out assessment can be found on pages 6 and 102 of this guide.

STATION - WEEK 10

Pencil Stencil

OBJECTIVES
–il

Spell and use words containing –il

Review previous learning

Ask the children if they can recall the spelling content and any examples from the previous spelling lesson. Elicit ideas and remind the children that: The sound /l/ or /el/ at the end of words can be spelt **le**, **el** and **al**, for example, **table**, **camel** and **metal**.

Introducing the rule

Explain to the children that in today's lesson they will learn about words that are spelt with **il** for the /l/ or /el/ sound at the end of words. There are not many words that end with **–il**.

Pupil Book Activity 1: Write it

1. Draw children's attention to the Word Bank at the top of page 20. Explain that all of these words contain the spelling pattern **il**.
2. Ask the children to read through the words in the Word Bank and talk to a partner about what they mean. Then ask the children if there are any words they are unsure of and explain the meanings to them, looking in the dictionary for a definition if necessary.
3. Model the activity by showing the children how to think of, say and write a sentence using the first word, **pupil**. Write your sentence on the board to show correct punctuation and handwriting formation. For example, say: What is a **pupil**? A pupil is a student but also a part of the eye. So my sentence could be 'The pupil worked hard in class'.
4. Ask the children to write a sentence for each of the given words. If children need some support, they could work in pairs to decide on a sentence and say it outloud before writing it. If children need full support, use these example answers to provide a dictated sentence (the adult reads the sentence and the children write it).

Example answers:

a) pupil: The pupil worked hard in class.

b) stencil: I drew a picture with the stencil.

c) utensil: I used the kitchen utensil when I was baking.

d) fossil: We found a fossil on the beach.

Pupil Book Activity 2: Crossword

1. Model the activity by reading the first clue aloud twice and then look through the Word Bank to find the correct answer.
2. Ask the children to read each clue, then find the answer words in the Word Bank and write them in the spaces provided.
3. Then ask the children to copy their answers into the correct places on the crossword. Explain that this is a way of checking if they have solved the clues correctly. The answers should fit into the crossword.

Answers: a) pencil; b) nostril; c) basil; d) April; e) gerbil

Pupil Book Activity 3: Choose a ditty

1. Ask the children to carefully read both ditties. Explain that when we want to remember how words are spelt, a useful method is to group them together into a fun ditty or phrase. When you think of one of the words in the ditty, you will automatically remember the other words that went with it.

2. The children could work independently or in pairs. Ask them to choose their favourite ditty and read it lots of times to try and learn it by heart. Challenge them to sing it to any simple melody.
3. Ask children to perform their ditty to the class by reciting or singing it.
4. As an extension to the task, you could also ask the children to find and underline the spelling patterns in the ditties, or draw a picture to illustrate one of them.

Ditties in this lesson:

A pupil put basil into the lentil soup and stirred it with the utensil.

In April we found a fossil and drew it using a pencil and a stencil.

Pupil Book Activity 4: Picture match

1. Remind the children of the Word Bank at the top of page 20.
2. Ask the children to find and copy words from the Word Bank to match the pictures.

Answers: a) pencil; b) nostril; c) gerbil; d) basil

Pupil Book Activity 5: Anagrams

1. Draw the children's attention to the anagrams in Activity 5. Explain to the children that the words have been taken from the Word Bank and the letters have been jumbled up into the wrong order.
2. Ask them to look carefully at the jumbled letters and try to work out which words from the Word Bank they are, then correctly write them in the space provided. Remind the children of the spelling patterns as a clue to help them: the letters **il** go together for the /l/ sound at the end of words.
3. As a method of self-checking, encourage the children to count how many letters are in the jumbled word and how many letters they have written in the correct spelling of the word to check that they are the same. If they aren't, suggest to the children that they check their spelling of the word.

Answers: a) evil; b) civil; c) pupil; d) nostril; e) utensil

Pupil Book Activity 6: Write a story

1. Set the children the challenge of writing their own short story using **il** words. Explain to the children that using the words in this way will help them to remember the words more effectively. Encourage the children to include as many of the Word Bank words as possible.
2. Use the following text as a model to show the children how to write the short story or, alternatively, use the text as a passage dictation by reading each sentence slowly and clearly for the children to write down:

The pupils were on a visit to the beach to look for fossils. They ate lentil soup on the train. They had packed pencils and stencils to draw the fossils. It was April and the weather was mild. Cassie had sneaked her gerbil into her jacket pocket.

Did you know?

1. Tell children that the –**le** spelling is the most common spelling for this sound at the end of words. The other ways of spelling it include **el**, **al** and **il**.

Assessment: il

Tell the children that you are going to read out ten words, one at a time. Each word will be one of the **il** words that they have been learning. Tell the children that you will say the word, and then you will read out a sentence containing the word to help them remember what it means. You will then repeat the word on its own again before pausing so that the children can write the word down. For example: **pencil**. I like to write in **pencil**. **pencil**

1. **pencil**. I like to write in **pencil**. **pencil**
2. **fossil**. We found a **fossil** in a rock. **fossil**
3. **nostril**. I have two **nostrils**. **nostril**
4. **gerbil**. I have a little pet **gerbil**. **gerbil**
5. **basil**. We added **basil** to the soup. **basil**
6. **evil**. The character was **evil**. **evil**
7. **pupil**. The **pupil** worked hard. **pupil**
8. **April**. It was the month of **April**. **April**
9. **stencil**. I used a **stencil** to draw. **stencil**
10. **utensil**. I stirred the soup with the **utensil**. **utensil**

For those students who need a little more of a spelling challenge, read out the further 'Quiet Zone' words to spell: **civil**, **lentil**

Full details of how to carry out assessment can be found on pages 6 and 102 of this guide.

STATION - WEEK 11

Dry July

OBJECTIVES
y /igh/
Spell and use words containing **igh**

Review previous learning

Ask the children if they can recall the spelling content and any examples from the previous spelling lesson. Elicit ideas and remind the children that: The sound /l/ or /el/ at the end of words can be spelt **il**, for example, **pencil**.

Introducing the rule

Explain to the children that in today's lesson they will learn about words that are spelt with –**y** at the end of words when it sounds like /igh/. The /igh/ sound can be spelt –**y** at the end of words. This is the most common spelling for this sound at the end of words.

> **Optional:** Review the Letterland character stories
>
> The Letterland stories help children to remember this spelling pattern (see page 115).

Pupil Book Activity 1: Fill the gaps

1. Draw children's attention to the Word Bank at the top of page 22. Explain that all of these words contain the spelling pattern –**y** for the /igh/ sound.
2. Ask the children to read through the words in the Word Bank and talk to a partner about what they mean. Then ask the children if there are any words they are unsure of and explain the meanings to them, looking in the dictionary for a definition if necessary.
3. Ask the children to read each clue, then find the answer words in the Word Bank and write them in the spaces provided.

Answers: a) sky; b) fly; c) July; d) sty; e) guy

Pupil Book Activity 3: Write it

1. Model the activity by showing the children how to think of, say and write a sentence using a word from the Word Bank, for example, **cry**. Write your sentence on the board to show correct punctuation and handwriting formation. For example, say: What does **cry** mean? Crying is what we do when we are very upset or hurt. So my sentence could be 'The sad story made me cry'.
2. Ask the children to write a sentence for two words chosen from each box. If children need some support, they could work in pairs to decide on the words, then create a sentence and say it outloud before writing it. If children need full support, use these example answers to provide a dictated sentence (the adult reads the sentence and the children write it).

Example answers:

a) July: I am going on holiday in July.

b) dry: The garden is dry without rain.

Pupil Book Activity 3: Choose a ditty

1. Ask the children to carefully read both ditties. Explain that when we want to remember how words are spelt, a useful method is to group them together into a fun ditty or phrase. When you think of one of the words in the ditty, you will automatically remember the other words that went with it.

2. The children could work independently or in pairs. Ask them to choose their favourite ditty and read it lots of times to try and learn it by heart. Challenge them to sing it to any simple melody.
3. Ask children to perform their ditty to the class by reciting or singing it.
4. As an extension to the task, you could also ask the children to find and underline the spelling patterns in the ditties, or draw a picture to illustrate one of them.

Ditties in this lesson:

Try not to cry in July when you see a fly in the sky.

Send a reply to the shy guy that is a spy standing by the sty.

Pupil Book Activity 4: Picture match

1. Remind the children of the Word Bank at the top of page 22.
2. Ask the children to find and copy words from the Word Bank to match the pictures.

Answers: a) fly; b) spy; c) sky; d) cry

Pupil Book Activity 5: Complete the passage

1. Read the passage to the children, pausing as you reach each gap. Complete the first gap with the children by re-reading to that point and then say: Look at the Word Bank. Which word is a game you can play? Elicit children's ideas and establish that the word is **spy** (I-Spy).
2. Ask the children to fill in the gaps in the rest of the passage independently or with a partner.

Answers: On the train the children played a game called I-**Spy**. Mum was taking them to a toyshop to **buy** a kite. It was a good day to **fly** a kite because the **sky** was blue with just the right amount of wind. It was the month of **July** and the grass at the park was **dry**. The children wanted to **try** and keep the kite up in the air for as long as they could.

Pupil Book Activity 6: Word search

1. Draw the children's attention to the word search at the bottom of page 23. Set the children the challenge of finding 6 -**y** /igh/ words in the word search. The words may be found horizontally from left to right or vertically from top to bottom.
2. Tell the children to circle each word as they find it and then write the words in the correct column.

Answers:

m	u	l	t	i	p	l	y
a	e	k	r	e	p	l	y
s	i	m	p	l	i	f	y
h	l	o	h	n	d	g	w
y	b	f	q	j	r	m	h
c	l	m	d	r	y	c	y

-**y** /igh/
multiply
reply
simplify
shy
why
dry

Assessment: y /igh/

Tell the children that you are going to read out twelve words, one at a time. Each word will be one of the **y** /igh/ words that they have been learning. Tell the children that you will say the word, and then you will read out a sentence containing the word to help them remember what it means. You will then repeat the word on its own again before pausing so that the children can write the word down. For example: **cry**. I **cry** when I feel sad. **cry**

1. **cry**. I **cry** when I feel sad. **cry**
2. **fly**. I watched a **fly** in the window. **fly**
3. **dry**. The grass is **dry**. **dry**
4. **try**. I always **try** my best. **try**
5. **reply**. I sent a **reply** to Gran. **reply**
6. **July**. My party is in **July**. **July**
7. **shy**. I often get **shy**. **shy**
8. **sky**. The **sky** was bright blue. **sky**
9. **spy**. My brother likes to **spy** on me. **spy**
10. **my**. I read **my** book. **my**
11. **by**. That story was written **by** me. **by**
12. **sty**. The pig sat in its **sty**. **sty**

For those students who need a little more of a spelling challenge, read out the six further 'Quiet Zone' words to spell: **fry, buy, guy, why, multiply, simplify**

Full details of how to carry out assessment can be found on pages 6 and 102 of this guide.

STATION - WEEK 12
Baby Bunnies

OBJECTIVES
-ies

Spell and use words containing plural ending -ies

Review previous learning

Ask the children if they can recall the spelling content and any examples from the previous spelling lesson. Elicit ideas and remind the children that: The /igh/ sound can be spelt **-y** at the end of words. This is the most common spelling for this sound at the end of words.

Introducing the rule

Explain to the children that in today's lesson they will learn about words that are spelt with **-ies** at the end. To add **-es** to nouns and verbs ending in **-y**, change the **-y** to an **i** before **-es** is added, for example, **lorry** + **es** = **lorries**.

Optional: Review the Letterland character stories

The Letterland stories help children to remember this spelling pattern (see page 115).

Optional: Review the Letterland Grammar analogies

Learn the analogy to help children understand plural noun suffixes (see page 118).

Pupil Book Activity 1: Add the endings

1. Draw children's attention to the Word Bank at the top of page 24. Explain that all of these words contain the spelling pattern **-ies**.
2. Ask the children to read through the words in the Word Bank and talk to a partner about what they mean. Then ask the children if there are any words they are unsure of and explain the meanings to them, looking in the dictionary for a definition if necessary.
3. Model the activity by demonstrating on the board how to add **-es** to one of the words from the activity, for example, **lady**. Write the word **lady** on the board then add **-es**: **ladyes** and place a cross next to it to show that this is incorrect. Write **lady** again and this time rub out the **y** to replace it with an **i** then add **es**: **ladies** and place a tick next to it to show that it is correct.
4. Ask the children to complete the chart by adding the ending correctly and remembering to change the **y** to an **i** each time.

Answers:

lorry	+ es	lorries
lady	+ es	ladies
baby	+ es	babies
berry	+ es	berries
fly	+ es	flies
cry	+ es	cries
try	+ es	tries
copy	+ es	copies

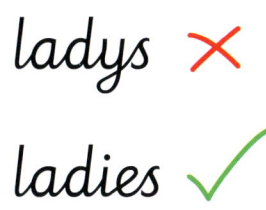

47

Pupil Book Activity 2: Crossword

1. Model the activity by reading the first clue aloud twice and then look through the Word Bank to find the correct answer.
2. Ask the children to read each clue, then find the answer words in the Word Bank and write them in the spaces provided.
3. Then ask the children to copy their answers into the correct places on the crossword. Explain that this is a way of checking if they have solved the clues correctly. The answers should fit into the crossword.

Answers: a) pennies; b) jellies; c) hobbies; d) replies; e) worries

Pupil Book Activity 3: Choose a ditty

1. Ask the children to carefully read both ditties. Explain that when we want to remember how words are spelt, a useful method is to group them together into a fun ditty or phrase. When you think of one of the words in the ditty, you will automatically remember the other words that went with it.
2. The children could work independently or in pairs. Ask them to choose their favourite ditty and read it lots of times to try and learn it by heart. Challenge them to sing it to any simple melody.
3. Ask children to perform their ditty to the class by reciting or singing it.
4. As an extension to the task, you could also ask the children to find and underline the spelling patterns in the ditties, or draw a picture to illustrate one of them.

Ditties in this lesson:

Ladies in lorries travel to cities to eat berries in jellies.

Babies and bunnies have no worries.

Pupil Book Activity 4: Picture match

1. Remind the children of the Word Bank at the top of page 24.
2. Ask the children to find and copy words from the Word Bank to match the pictures.

Answers: a) lorries; b) bunnies; c) ladies; d) pennies

Pupil Book Activity 5: Anagrams

1. Draw the children's attention to the anagrams in Activity 5. Explain to the children that the words have been taken from the Word Bank and the letters have been jumbled up into the wrong order.
2. Ask them to look carefully at the jumbled letters and try to work out which words from the Word Bank they are, then correctly write them in the space provided. Remind the children of the spelling patterns as a clue to help them: the letters **ies** will be together at the end of the words.
3. As a method of self-checking, encourage the children to count how many letters are in the jumbled word and how many letters they have written in the correct spelling of the word to check that they are the same. If they aren't, suggest to the children that they check their spelling of the word.

Answers: a) dries; b) flies; c) berries; d) babies; e) copies

Pupil Book Activity 6: Write a story

1. Set the children the challenge of writing their own short story using **-ies** words. Explain to the children that using the words in this way will help them to remember the words more effectively. Encourage the children to include as many of the Word Bank words as possible.
2. Use the following text as a model to show the children how to write the short story or, alternatively, use the text as a passage dictation by reading each sentence slowly and clearly for the children to write down:

The station was very busy. There was a big queue of ladies with their babies. Lots of the babies were cuddling toy bunnies. The ladies tried to stop their cries by pulling funny faces.

Assessment: -ies

Tell the children that you are going to read out twelve words, one at a time. Each word will be one of the **-ies** words that they have been learning. Tell the children that you will say the word, and then you will read out a sentence containing the word to help them remember what it means. You will then repeat the word on its own again before pausing so that the children can write the word down. For example:
lorries. I saw a queue of **lorries**. **lorries**

1. **lorries**. I saw a queue of **lorries**. **lorries**
2. **ladies**. Mum went to lunch with the **ladies**. **ladies**
3. **babies**. The pool was full of **babies**. **babies**
4. **berries**. The birds pecked at the **berries**. **berries**
5. **pennies**. I counted all my **pennies**. **pennies**
6. **worries**. I try to forget my **worries**. **worries**
7. **bunnies**. The **bunnies** hop about in the fields. **bunnies**
8. **flies**. The plane **flies** past my house every day. **flies**
9. **cries**. We heard **cries** coming from upstairs. **cries**
10. **tries**. Fred **tries** his best. **tries**
11. **replies**. We got five **replies** to the party invitations. **replies**
12. **dries**. The sun **dries** the wet clothes. **dries**

For those students who need a little more of a spelling challenge, read out the further 'Quiet Zone' words to spell: **hobbies**, **cities**, **copies**, **jellies**

Full details of how to carry out assessment can be found on pages 6 and 102 of this guide.

STATION - WEEK 13

Happy Happier

OBJECTIVES
Suffixes on –y words
Spell and use words containing the suffixes
–ing, –ed, –er, –est

Review previous learning

Ask the children if they can recall the spelling content and any examples from the previous spelling lesson. Elicit ideas and remind the children that: To add –**es** to nouns and verbs ending in –**y**, change the –**y** to an **i** before –**es** is added, for example, **lorry** + **es** = **lorries**.

Introducing the rule

Explain to the children that in today's lesson they will learn about words that are spelt with –**ing**, –**ed**, –**er** and –**est** at the end. When adding –**ed**, –**er** and –**est** to a root word ending in –**y** with a consonant before it, change the –**y** to an **i**. When adding –**ing**, don't change the **y** to an **i** as this would result in **ii**. The only ordinary words with **ii** are **skiing** and **taxiing**.

Optional: Review the Letterland character stories

The Letterland stories help children to remember this spelling pattern (see page 115).

Optional: Review the Letterland Grammar analogies

Learn the analogy to help children understand suffixes (see page 118).

Pupil Book Activity 1: Add the endings

1. Draw children's attention to the Word Bank at the top of page 26. Explain that all of these words contain the spelling patterns –**ing**, –**ed**, –**er**, and –**est** at the end.
2. Ask the children to read through the words in the Word Bank and talk to a partner about what they mean. Then ask the children if there are any words they are unsure of and explain the meanings to them, looking in the dictionary for a definition if necessary.
3. Model the activity by demonstrating on the board how to add –**ing** and –**ed** to one of the words from the activity, for example, **carry**. Write the word **carry** on the board then add –**ing**: **carrying** and place a tick next to it to show that this is correct. Write **carry** again and this time rub out the **y** to replace it with an **i** then add –**ed**: **carried** and place a tick next to it to show that it is correct.
4. Ask the children to complete the chart by adding the ending correctly and remembering to change the **y** to an **i** each time it is needed for the –**ed** ending.

Answers:

root word	-ing	-ed
carry	carrying	carried
cry	crying	cried
reply	replying	replied
study	studying	studied
hurry	hurrying	hurried
copy	copying	copied
supply	supplying	supplied
empty	emptying	emptied

carry

carrying ✓

carried ✓

Pupil Book Activity 2: Write it

1. Model the activity by showing the children how to think of, say and write a sentence using a word from the Word Bank, for example, **carried**. Write your sentence on the board to show correct punctuation and handwriting formation. For example, say: What does **carried** mean? It means you lifted and moved something. So my sentence could be 'I carried the shopping bags into the house'.
2. Ask the children to write a sentence for two words chosen from the Word Bank. If children need some support, they could work in pairs to decide on the words, then create a sentence and say it outloud before writing it. If children need full support, use these example answers to provide a dictated sentence (the adult reads the sentence and the children write it).

Example answers:

a) happier: I have never been happier than today.

b) emptying: I was busy emptying the bins.

Pupil Book Activity 3: Choose a ditty

1. Ask the children to carefully read both ditties. Explain that when we want to remember how words are spelt, a useful method is to group them together into a fun ditty or phrase. When you think of one of the words in the ditty, you will automatically remember the other words that went with it.
2. The children could work independently or in pairs. Ask them to choose their favourite ditty and read it lots of times to try and learn it by heart. Challenge them to sing it to any simple melody.
3. Ask children to perform their ditty to the class by reciting or singing it.
4. As an extension to the task, you could also ask the children to find and underline the spelling patterns in the ditties, or draw a picture to illustrate one of them.

Ditties in this lesson:

The funniest clown was crying as he carried the prettiest bucket.

It was chillier outside but I had never felt happier or sillier.

Pupil Book Activity 4: Add the endings

1. Model the activity by demonstrating on the board how to add –**er** and -**est** to one of the words from the activity, for example, **happy**. Write the word **happy** on the board then rub out the **y** to replace it with an **i** before adding –**er**: **happier** and place a tick next to it to show that this is correct. Write **happy** again and rub out the **y** to replace it with an **i** then add –**est**: **happiest** and place a tick next to it to show that it is correct.
2. Ask the children to complete the chart by adding the ending correctly and remembering to change the **y** to an **i** each time it is needed for the –**er** and –**est** endings.

Answers:

root word	-er	-est
happy	happier	happiest
lucky	luckier	luckiest
chilly	chillier	chilliest
lazy	lazier	laziest
pretty	prettier	prettiest
funny	funnier	funniest
silly	sillier	silliest
busy	busier	busiest

happy

happier ✓

happiest ✓

Pupil Book Activity 5: Complete the passage

1. Read the passage to the children, pausing as you reach each gap. Complete the first gap with the children by re-reading to that point and then say: Look at the words in the box. Which word describes how a day could be? Elicit children's ideas and establish that the word is **chilliest**.
2. Ask the children to fill in the gaps in the rest of the passage independently or with a partner.

Answers: It was the <u>chilliest</u> day so far this winter. Robert and Sam felt like the <u>luckiest</u> boys on the train. They were <u>happier</u> than they had been all week. The train driver had invited them to the front! They <u>carried</u> their bags and <u>hurried</u> to the front of the train. There they saw the <u>busiest</u> control panel they had ever seen.

Pupil Book Activity 6: Word search

1. Draw the children's attention to the word search at the bottom of page 27. Set the children the challenge of finding 6 –**ing** and –**ed** words in the word search. The words may be found horizontally from left to right.
2. Tell the children to circle each word as they find it and then write the words in the correct column.

Answers:

c	a	r	r	y	i	n	g
a	h	u	r	r	i	e	d
p	c	r	y	i	n	g	r
e	m	p	t	i	e	d	s
f	r	e	p	l	i	e	d
c	o	p	y	i	n	g	t

–ing	–ed
carrying	hurried
crying	emptied
copying	replied

Assessment: –ing, –ed, –er, –est to –y words

Tell the children that you are going to read out twelve words, one at a time. Each word will be one of the –**ing**, –**ed**, –**er** or –**est** words that they have been learning. Tell the children that you will say the word, and then you will read out a sentence containing the word to help them remember what it means. You will then repeat the word on its own again before pausing so that the children can write the word down. For example: **crying**. Mum kept **crying** during the film. **crying**

1. **crying**. Mum kept **crying** during the film. **crying**
2. **carried**. I **carried** my bag to the car. **carried**
3. **happier**. I was **happier** when my cat came back. **happier**
4. **hurried**. We **hurried** because we were late. **hurried**
5. **copying**. I was **copying** the words. **copying**
6. **funniest**. My sister is the **funniest** girl. **funniest**
7. **emptying**. I was **emptying** the bin. **emptying**
8. **sillier**. We became sillier and **sillier**. **sillier**
9. **busiest**. The town is **busiest** in the morning. **busiest**
10. **copied**. I **copied** the answers to check. **copied**
11. **lazier**. My dog gets **lazier** by the day. **lazier**
12. **laziest**. My big brother is the **laziest** family member. **laziest**

For those students who need a little more of a spelling challenge, read out the six further 'Quiet Zone' words to spell: **studying, supplied, luckiest, replied, chillier, prettier**

STATION - WEEK 14

Stripy Hiker

OBJECTIVES
Suffixes on **e** words

Spell and use words containing the suffixes **-ed, -ing, -er, -est, -y**

Review previous learning

Ask the children if they can recall the spelling content and any examples from the previous spelling lesson. Elicit ideas and remind the children that: When adding **-ed**, **-er** and **-est** to a root word ending in **-y** with a consonant before it, change the **-y** to an **i**.

Introducing the rule

Explain to the children that in today's lesson they will learn about words that are spelt with **-ing**, **-ed**, **-er**, **-est** and **-y** at the end. When adding **-ing**, **-ed**, **-er**, **-est** or **-y** to words ending in **-e** with a consonant before it, drop the **e**, for example, **arrive + ing = arriving**.

Pupil Book Activity 1: Add the endings

1. Draw children's attention to the Word Bank at the top of page 28. Explain that all of these words contain the spelling patterns **-ing**, **-ed**, **-er**, **-est** and **-y** at the end.
2. Ask the children to read through the words in the Word Bank and talk to a partner about what they mean. Then ask the children if there are any words they are unsure of and explain the meanings to them, looking in the dictionary for a definition if necessary.
3. Model the activity by demonstrating on the board how to add **-ing** and **-ed** to one of the words from the activity, for example, **arrive**. Write the word **arrive** on the board then rub out the **e** and add **-ing**: **arriving** and place a tick next to it to show that this is correct. Write **arrive** again and rub out the **e** to add **-ed**: **arrived** and place a tick next to it to show that it is correct.
4. Ask the children to complete the chart by adding the ending correctly and remembering to remove the end **e** each time.

Answers:

root word	-ing	-ed
arrive	arriving	arrived
excite	exciting	excited
invite	inviting	invited
move	moving	moved
slice	slicing	sliced
slide	sliding	slid*
sneeze	sneezing	sneezed
wipe	wiping	wiped

*Explain that slide becomes **slid** instead of **slided**.

Pupil Book Activity 2: Anagrams

1. Draw the children's attention to the anagrams in Activity 2. Explain to the children that the words have been taken from the Word Bank and the letters have been jumbled up into the wrong order.
2. Ask them to look carefully at the jumbled letters and try to work out which words from the Word Bank they are, then correctly write them in the space provided. Remind the children of the spelling

patterns as a clue to help them: the endings of the words will be –**ing**, –**ed**, –**er**, –**est** or –**y**.

3. As a method of self-checking, encourage the children to count how many letters are in the jumbled word and how many letters they have written in the correct spelling of the word to check that they are the same. If they aren't, suggest to the children that they check their spelling of the word.

Answers: a) nicer; b) noisy; c) moving; d) wiped; e) wisest

Pupil Book Activity 3: Add the endings

1. Model the activity by demonstrating on the board how to add –**y** to one of the words from the activity, for example, **ice**. Write the word ice on the board then rub out the **e** to replace it with the ending –**y**: icy and place a tick next to it to show that this is correct.
2. Ask the children to complete the chart by adding the ending correctly and remembering to remove the end **e** when adding the –**y**.

Answers:

root word	-y
ice	icy
juice	juicy
noise	noisy
nose	nosy*
scare	scary
shine	shiny

*You might wish to mention that the alternative spelling 'nosey' is also considered acceptable.

Pupil Book Activity 4: Add the endings

1. Model the activity by demonstrating on the board how to add –**er** and –**est** to one of the words from the activity, for example, **brave**. Write the word **brave** on the board then rub out the **e** before adding –**er**: **braver** and place a tick next to it to show that this is correct. Write **brave** again and rub out the **e** then add –**est**: **bravest** and place a tick next to it to show that it is correct.
2. Ask the children to complete the chart by adding the –**er** and –**est** endings.

Answers:

root word	-er	-est
brave	braver	bravest
close	closer	closest
fierce	fiercer	fiercest
gentle	gentler	gentlest
large	larger	largest
nice	nicer	nicest
wise	wiser	wisest

Pupil Book Activity 5: Choose a ditty

1. Ask the children to carefully read both ditties. Explain that when we want to remember how words are spelt, a useful method is to group them together into a fun ditty or phrase. When you think of one of the words in the ditty, you will automatically remember the other words that went with it.
2. The children could work independently or in pairs. Ask them to choose their favourite ditty and read

it lots of times to try and learn it by heart. Challenge them to sing it to any simple melody.
3. Ask children to perform their ditty to the class by reciting or singing it.
4. As an extension to the task, you could also ask the children to find and underline the spelling patterns in the ditties, or draw a picture to illustrate one of them.

Ditties in this lesson:

The mouse was braver, wiser and nicer than the lion.

Jim was excited that he was invited to the noisy disco.

Pupil Book Activity 6: Write a story

1. Set the children the challenge of writing their own short story using **-ing**, **-ed**, **-er**, **-est**, and **-y** words. Explain to the children that using the words in this way will help them to remember the words more effectively. Encourage the children to include as many of the Word Bank words as possible.
2. Use the following text as a model to show the children how to write the short story or, alternatively, use the text as a passage dictation by reading each sentence slowly and clearly for the children to write down:

Kevin arrived at the station just as he finished eating a juicy pear. Mum said he was the bravest boy she knew. He thought it was all quite exciting. The time was getting closer. He had been invited to meet a tarantula. It was the fiercest creature he had ever met but when he saw it moving, he realised it was far gentler than he had thought it would be.

Did you know?

Tell the children that the exception to the spelling rule is 'being'.

Assessment: –ing, –ed, –er, –est, –y to –e words

Tell the children that you are going to read out twelve words, one at a time. Each word will be one of the **-ing**, **-ed**, **-er**, **-est** or **-y** words that they have been learning. Tell the children that you will say the word, and then you will read out a sentence containing the word to help them remember what it means. You will then repeat the word on its own again before pausing so that the children can write the word down. For example: **bravest**. I am the **bravest** in my family. **bravest**

1. **bravest**. I am the **bravest** in my family. **bravest**
2. **exciting**. It is so **exciting** to get a new pet. **exciting**
3. **closer**. I have moved house to be **closer** to school. **closer**
4. **invited**. We were **invited** to dinner. **invited**
5. **wiped**. I **wiped** the table clean. **wiped**
6. **stripy**. My brother's jumper is **stripy**. **stripy**
7. **largest**. I drank the **largest** milkshake. **largest**
8. **sneezed**. I **sneezed** when the door opened. **sneezed**
9. **nicer**. We gave Nan some **nicer** flowers. **nicer**
10. **sliding**. I love **sliding** down the slide. **sliding**
11. **wisest**. My Grandpa is the **wisest** person I know. **wisest**
12. **shiny**. I have a **shiny** coin. **shiny**

For those students who need a little more of a spelling challenge, read out the six further 'Quiet Zone' words to spell: **fiercest**, **gentler**, **moving**, **juicy**, **noisy**, **arrived**

STATION - WEEK 15

Humming Runner

OBJECTIVES

-ing, -ed, -er, -est, -y

Suffixes added to one syllable single vowel words

Review previous learning

Ask the children if they can recall the spelling content and any examples from the previous spelling lesson. Elicit ideas and remind the children that: When adding **-ing**, **-ed**, **-er**, **-est** or **-y** to words ending in **-e** with a consonant before it, drop the **e**, for example, **arrive** + **ing** = **arriving**.

Introducing the rule

Explain to the children that in today's lesson they will learn about words that are spelt with **-ing**, **-ed**, **-er**, **-est** and **-y** at the end. When adding these suffixes to words of one syllable ending in a single consonant letter after a single vowel letter, double the last consonant letter to keep the vowel sound short.

Optional: Review the Letterland character stories

The story about 'Best Friends to the Rescue' explains these spelling patterns (see page 115).

Optional: Review the Letterland Grammar analogies

Learn the analogy to help children understand suffixes (see page 118).

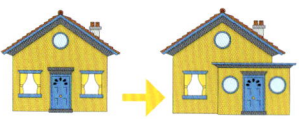

Pupil Book Activity 1: Add the endings

1. Draw children's attention to the Word Bank at the top of page 30. Explain that all of these words contain the spelling patterns **-ing**, **-ed**, **-er**, **-est** and **-y** at the end.

2. Ask the children to read through the words in the Word Bank and talk to a partner about what they mean. Then ask the children if there are any words they are unsure of and explain the meanings to them, looking in the dictionary for a definition if necessary.

3. Model the activity by demonstrating on the board how to add **-ing** and **-ed** to one of the words from the activity, for example, **pat**. Write the word **pat** on the board then add the ending **-ing**. Read the word aloud 'pating' to show that without the double consonant letter the **a** has become a long vowel sound. Rub out the **ing** ending and double the consonant before adding **-ing** again: **patting** and place a tick next to it to show that this is correct. Write **pat** again and double the **t** again before adding **-ed**: **patted** and place a tick next to it to show that it is correct.

4. Ask the children to complete the chart by adding the ending correctly and remembering to remove the end **e** each time.

Answers:

root word	consonant +ing	consonant +ed
pat	patting	patted
hum	humming	hummed
drop	dropping	dropped
chat	chatting	chatted
slip	slipping	slipped
hop	hopping	hopped
skip	skipping	skipped
stop	stopping	stopped

pat

pating ✗

patting ✓

patted ✓

Pupil Book Activity 2: Anagrams

1. Draw the children's attention to the anagrams in Activity 2. Explain to the children that the words have been taken from the Word Bank and the letters have been jumbled up into the wrong order.
2. Ask them to look carefully at the jumbled letters and try to work out which words from the Word Bank they are, then correctly write them in the space provided. Remind the children of the spelling patterns as a clue to help them: the letters at the end of the words will be either **–ing**, **–ed**, **–er**, **–est** or **–y**.
3. As a method of self-checking, encourage the children to count how many letters are in the jumbled word and how many letters they have written in the correct spelling of the word to check that they are the same. If they aren't, suggest to the children that they check their spelling of the word.

Answers: a) hotter; b) chatted; c) patting; d) sadder; e) mummy

Pupil Book Activity 3: Add more endings

1. Model the activity by demonstrating on the board how to add **–y** to one of the words from the activity, for example, **run**. Write the word **run** on the board then demonstrate the need to double the consonant **n** before adding the ending **–y**: **runny** and place a tick next to it to show that this is correct.
1. Ask the children to complete the chart by adding the ending correctly and remembering to double the final consonant when adding the **–y**.

Answers:

root word	consonant + y
run	runny
fun	funny
mud	muddy
dad	daddy
mum	mummy

Pupil Book Activity 4: Add more endings

1. Model the activity by demonstrating on the board how to add **–er** and **–est** to one of the words from the activity, for example, **sad**. Write the word **sad** on the board then double the final consonant before adding **–er**: **sadder** and place a tick next to it to show that this is correct. Write **sad** again and double the **d** before adding **–est**: **saddest** and place a tick next to it to show that it is correct.
2. Ask the children to complete the chart by adding the ending correctly and remembering to double the final consonant each time before adding the **–er** and **–est** endings.

Answers:

root word	consonant +er	consonant +est
sad	sadder	saddest
fat	fatter	fattest
big	bigger	biggest
thin	thinner	thinnest
hot	hotter	hottest

Pupil Book Activity 5: Choose a ditty

1. Ask the children to carefully read both ditties. Explain that when we want to remember how words are spelt, a useful method is to group them together into a fun ditty or phrase. When you think of one of the words in the ditty, you will automatically remember the other words that went with it.
2. The children could work independently or in pairs. Ask them to choose their favourite ditty and read it lots of times to try and learn it. Challenge them to sing it and perform it to any simple melody.
3. As an extension to the task, you could also ask the children to find and underline the spelling patterns in the ditties, or draw a picture to illustrate one of them.

Ditties in this lesson:

We ate the biggest, thinnest, hottest pizza.

Daddy got muddy when he skipped and slipped.

Pupil Book Activity 6: Write a story

1. Set the children the challenge of writing their own short story using –**ing**, –**ed**, –**er**, –**est** and –**y** words. Explain to the children that using the words in this way will help them to remember the words more effectively. Encourage the children to include as many of the Word Bank words as possible.
2. Use the following text as a model to show the children how to write the short story or, alternatively, use the text as a passage dictation by reading each sentence slowly and clearly for the children to write down:

Mummy laughed when Daddy told her a funny joke. They hopped onto the train and stopped to sit down near the window. Mummy hummed a tune while Daddy rubbed his belly, which was full from dinner. They chatted all the way home.

Did you know?

1. Tell the children that the letter **x** is never doubled and show the examples: **mixing**, **mixed**, **boxer**, **sixes**.

Assessment: –ing, –ed, –er, –est, –y to one syllable single vowel words

Tell the children that you are going to read out twelve words, one at a time. Each word will be one of the –**ing**, –**ed**, –**er**, –**est** or –**y** words that they have been learning. Tell the children that you will say the word, and then you will read out a sentence containing the word to help them remember what it means. You will then repeat the word on its own again before pausing so that the children can write the word down. For example: **patting**. Kim was **patting** the dog. **patting**

1. **patting**. Kim was **patting** the dog. **patting**
2. **runny**. I like my eggs **runny** in the middle. **runny**
3. **sadder**. I have never been **sadder**. **sadder**
4. **funny**. My cat is so **funny**. **funny**
5. **dropping**. I was **dropping** the bags because they were heavy. **dropping**
6. **bigger**. My feet are growing **bigger**. **bigger**
7. **muddy**. We stomped in the **muddy** puddles. **muddy**
8. **daddy**. William showed his **daddy** the new book. **daddy**
9. **slipping**. We were **slipping** all over the place. **slipping**
10. **mummy**. Tina heard her **mummy** talking. **mummy**
11. **skipping**. We were all **skipping** with joy. **skipping**
12. **hotter**. The temperature was getting **hotter**. **hotter**

For those students who need a little more of a spelling challenge, read out the six further 'Quiet Zone' words to spell: **hummed**, **thinnest**, **hopped**, **stopped**, **fatter**, **chatted**

STATION - WEEK 16

Wild Plant

STATION RULE
Some words do not sound the way you might expect them to. Pay attention to which parts of the word you know and which parts are tricky.

Review previous learning

Ask the children if they can recall the spelling rule or any example words from the previous spelling lesson. Elicit ideas and remind the children that: When adding **–ing**, **–ed**, **–er**, **–est** or **-y** to words of one syllable ending in a single consonant letter after a single vowel letter, double the last consonant letter to keep the vowel sound short.

Introducing the rule

Explain to the children that in today's lesson they will learn about words that can be difficult to spell because the letter-sound correspondences in them have not yet been taught, but the words are so useful that we want to use them now.

Some words do not sound the way you might expect them to. Pay attention to which parts of the word you know and which parts are tricky.

Pupil Book Activity 1: Read the Word Bank and the Example Sentences

1. Draw the children's attention to the Word Bank in the left-hand column of page 32. Explain that all of these words contain parts that have not yet been taught but that it is likely the children will know how to read the words from encountering them in reading books.
2. Ask the children to read through the words in the Word Bank and talk to a partner about what they mean. Then ask the children if there are any words they are unsure of and explain the meanings to them, looking in the dictionary for a definition if necessary.
3. Ask the children to read the example sentences in the second column to help them understand the words in context.

Pupil Book Activity 2: Colour the parts

1. Draw the children's attention to the third column which contains the words shown so that each phoneme (sound) is distinguishable.
2. Ask the children to say the sounds while thinking carefully about the whole word. Remind them that the letters may not sound the way they expect.
3. Ask the children to colour the easy parts of the word in green and the tricky parts in orange. For example, in the words 'find', 'kind' and 'mind' the letter **i** represents an /igh/ sound. Alternatively ask them to write a wiggly line underneath the tricky part.

Pupil Book Activity 3: Write the word

1. In the final column, ask the children to write each word. If they feel confident, they could cover up the information in the other columns. If they lack confidence, they should copy the spelling from the other columns and say the word as they write it.
2. Remind the children to look back through their spellings to check for accuracy.

Assessment: Tricky Words

Tell the children that you are going to read out twentyone words, one at a time. Each word will be one of the tricky words that they have been learning. Tell the children that you will say the word, and then you will read out a sentence containing the word to help them remember what it means. You will then repeat the word on its own again before pausing so that the children can write the word down.

For example: **door**. I opened the door. **door**

1. **door**. I opened the **door**. **door**
2. **floor**. I swept the **floor**. **floor**
3. **poor**. My **poor** teddy has a torn ear. **poor**
4. **find**. I always **find** coins under the sofa. **find**
5. **kind**. My sister was **kind** to share. **kind**
6. **mind**. I have a lot on my **mind**. **mind**
7. **behind**. Try not to get left **behind**. **behind**
8. **child**. There is a new **child** in our class. **child**
9. **wild**. We saw a **wild** rabbit. **wild**
10. **most**. I ate **most** of my sandwich. **most**
11. **only**. I **only** like green apples. **only**
12. **both**. I like **both** green and red apples. **both**
13. **old**. My mum's car is **old**. **old**
14. **cold**. I think I've caught a **cold**. **cold**
15. **gold**. The pirates were digging for **gold**. **gold**
16. **hold**. I asked to **hold** the baby. **hold**
17. **told**. I **told** a little lie. **told**
18. **every**. I read my book **every** day. **every**
19. **everybody**. I invited **everybody** to my party. **everybody**
20. **even**. I **even** invited my gran. **even**
21. **plant**. I must remember to water that **plant**. **plant**

For those students who need a little more of a spelling challenge, read out the further 'Quiet Zone' words to spell: **pretty**, **climb**, **great**, **break**, **steak**, **because**, **children**

Full details of how to carry out assessment can be found on pages 6 and 102 of this guide.

STATION - WEEK 17

Small Stall

OBJECTIVES
–al –all

/or/ sound is usually spelt as a before l and ll

Review previous learning

Ask the children if they can recall the spelling content and any examples from the previous spelling lesson. Elicit ideas and remind the children that they were learning about words that can be difficult to spell because the letter-sound correspondences in them have not yet been taught, but the words are so useful that we want to use them now, for example, **because** and **behind**.

Introducing the rule

Explain to the children that in today's lesson they will learn about words that are spelt with **all** and **al** for the /or/ sound.

The /or/ sound is usually spelt as **a** before **l** and **ll**, for example, **walk** and **ball**.

Optional: Review the Letterland story

To help, you might like to talk about Giant All, who lives in Letterland and steals all the apples!

Pupil Book Activity 1: Sort it

1. Draw children's attention to the Word Bank at the top of page 34. Explain that all of these words contain the spelling patterns **al** and **all**.
2. Ask the children to read through the words in the Word Bank and talk to a partner about what they mean. Then ask the children if there are any words they are unsure of and explain the meanings to them, looking in the dictionary for a definition if necessary.
3. Ask the children to sort and write each word into the correct box according to the spelling pattern it contains.

Answers:

all	al
small	stalk
stall	
ball	walk
call	
tall	always
fall	
smallest	talk
calling	
taller	walked

Pupil Book Activity 2: Crossword

1. Model the activity by reading the first clue aloud twice and then look through the Word Bank to find the correct answer.
2. Ask the children to read each clue, then find the answer words in the Word Bank and write them in the spaces provided.
3. Then ask the children to copy their answers into the correct places on the crossword. Explain that this is a way of checking if they have solved the clues correctly. The answers should fit into the crossword.
Answers: a) ball; b) stalk; c) small; d) stall; e) fall

Pupil Book Activity 3: Choose a ditty

1. Ask the children to carefully read both ditties. Explain that when we want to remember how words are spelt, a useful method is to group them together into a fun ditty or phrase. When you think of one of the words in the ditty, you will automatically remember the other words that went with it.
2. The children could work independently or in pairs. Ask them to choose their favourite ditty and read it lots of times to try and learn it by heart. Challenge them to sing it to any simple melody.
3. Ask children to perform their ditty to the class by reciting or singing it.
4. As an extension to the task, you could also ask the children to find and underline the spelling patterns in the ditties, or draw a picture to illustrate one of them.

Ditties in this lesson:

We always talk while we walk and throw a small ball.

Call the stall and ask if they have a plant with a tall stalk.

Pupil Book Activity 4: Picture match

1. Remind the children of the Word Bank at the top of page 34.
2. Ask the children to find and copy words from the Word Bank to match the pictures.

Answers: a) stalk; b) talk; c) stall; d) ball

Pupil Book Activity 5: Anagrams

3. Draw the children's attention to the anagrams in Activity 5. Explain to the children that the words have been taken from the Word Bank and the letters have been jumbled up into the wrong order.
4. Ask them to look carefully at the jumbled letters and try to work out which words from the Word Bank they are, then correctly write them in the space provided. Remind the children of the spelling patterns as a clue to help them: the letter **a** will be followed by **l** or **ll**.
5. As a method of self-checking, encourage the children to count how many letters are in the jumbled word and how many letters they have written in the correct spelling of the word to check that they are the same. If they aren't, suggest to the children that they check their spelling of the word.

Answers: a) calling; b) smallest; c) taller; d) fall; e) always

Pupil Book Activity 6: Write a story

1. Set the children the challenge of writing their own short story using **all** and **al** words. Explain to the children that using the words in this way will help them to remember the words more effectively. Encourage the children to include as many of the Word Bank words as possible.
2. Use the following text as a model to show the children how to write the short story or, alternatively, use the text as a passage dictation by reading each sentence slowly and clearly for the children to write down:
Wendy and Nan walked along the station platform. Wendy noticed some small stalks poking up out of the ground by the tracks. "Don't worry," said Nan, "Those stalks always pop up there but they never get very tall." At that moment, Nan spotted Viv who had just stepped off the train. Nan called her over and they talked about Viv's journey.

Assessment: all, al

Tell the children that you are going to read out ten words, one at a time. Each word will be one of the **all** or **al** words that they have been learning. Tell the children that you will say the word, and then you will read out a sentence containing the word to help them remember what it means. You will then repeat the word on its own again before pausing so that the children can write the word down. For example: **small**. My baby brother is **small**. **small**

1. **small**. My baby brother is **small**. **small**
2. **stall**. We bought eggs from the market **stall**. **stall**
3. **stalk**. I cut the flower **stalk**. **stalk**
4. **ball**. My puppy loves to play with a **ball**. **ball**
5. **call**. I **call** my big sister to come for dinner. **call**
6. **walk**. My family loves to go on a **walk**. **walk**
7. **tall**. Nan says I am getting **tall**. **tall**
8. **always**. We **always** listen to the radio in the morning. **always**
9. **fall**. My grandfather had a **fall**. **fall**
10. **talk**. I heard my mum **talk** to my teacher. **talk**

For those students who need a little more of a spelling challenge, read out the further 'Quiet Zone' words to spell: **smallest**, **calling**, **walked**, **taller**

Full details of how to carry out assessment can be found on pages 6 and 102 of this guide.

STATION - WEEK 18
Honey Love

OBJECTIVES
o /u/ sound

Spell and use words containing o /u/

Review previous learning

Ask the children if they can recall the spelling content and any examples from the previous spelling lesson. Elicit ideas and remind the children that: the /or/ sound is usually spelt as **a** before **l** and **ll**, for example, **walk** and **ball**.

Introducing the rule

Explain to the children that in today's lesson they will learn about words that are spelt with **o** for the /u/ sound.

The /u/ sound is sometimes spelt as **o**, for example, **honey** and **mother**.

Optional: Review the Letterland story

To help, you might like to talk about Oscar's Bothersome Little Brother (see page 115).

Pupil Book Activity 1: Crossword

1. Draw children's attention to the Word Bank at the top of page 36. Explain that all of these words contain the spelling pattern **o** for the /u/ sound.
2. Ask the children to read through the words in the Word Bank and talk to a partner about what they mean. Then ask the children if there are any words they are unsure of and explain the meanings to them, looking in the dictionary for a definition if necessary.
3. Ask the children to read each clue, then find the answer words in the Word Bank and write them in the spaces provided.

Answers: a) Monday; b) oven; c) dozen; d) honey; e) glove

Pupil Book Activity 2: Write it

1. Model the activity by showing the children how to think of, say and write a sentence using a word from the Word Bank, for example, **honey**. Write your sentence on the board to show correct punctuation and handwriting formation. For example, say: What is **honey**? It's sweet and sticky, made by bees and we eat it. So my sentence could be 'I like to put honey on my toast.'
2. Ask the children to write a sentence for two words from the Word Bank. If children need some support, they could work in pairs to decide on a sentence and say it outloud before writing it. If children need full support, use these example answers to provide a dictated sentence (the adult reads the sentence and the children write it).

Example answers:

a) honey: I like to put honey on my toast.

b) love: I love playing tennis.

c) brother: My brother is called Jim.

d) Monday: I am going swimming on Monday.

e) another: We are getting another pet fish.

Pupil Book Activity 3: Choose a ditty

1. Ask the children to carefully read both ditties. Explain that when we want to remember how words are spelt, a useful method is to group them together into a fun ditty or phrase. When you think of one of the words in the ditty, you will automatically remember the other words that went with it.
2. The children could work independently or in pairs. Ask them to choose their favourite ditty and read it lots of times to try and learn it by heart. Challenge them to sing it to any simple melody.
3. Ask children to perform their ditty to the class by reciting or singing it.
4. As an extension to the task, you could also ask the children to find and underline the spelling patterns in the ditties, or draw a picture to illustrate one of them.

Ditties in this lesson:

Mother put a dozen honey-covered cookies in the oven.

My brother and I love doing nothing on a Monday.

Pupil Book Activity 4: Picture match

1. Remind the children of the Word Bank at the top of page 36.
2. Ask the children to find and copy words from the Word Bank to match the pictures.

Answers: a) honey; b) glove; c) oven; d) dozen

Pupil Book Activity 5: Complete the passage

1. Read the passage to the children, pausing as you reach each gap. Complete the first gap with the children by re-reading to that point and then say: Look at the Word Bank. Which word might use the word 'on' before it? Elicit children's ideas and establish that the word is **Monday**.
2. Ask the children to fill in the gaps in the rest of the passage independently or with a partner.

Answers: On **Monday** my **brother** lost his black **glove** at the station. **Mother** looked for it and found **another** one that was not his. He was sad because he **loved** that pair. We checked the lost property but there was **nothing**.

Pupil Book Activity 6: Word search

1. Draw the children's attention to the word search at the bottom of page 37. Set the children the challenge of finding 6 **o** /u/ words in the word search. The words may be found horizontally from left to right or vertically from top to bottom.
2. Tell the children to circle each word as they find it and then write the words in the column.

Answers:

d	o	z	e	n	e	d
l	h	o	n	e	y	f
b	g	a	l	o	v	e
s	o	n	k	h	i	p
c	o	v	e	r	v	e
n	o	t	h	i	n	g

o
dozen
honey
love
son
cover
nothing

Assessment: o /u/

Tell the children that you are going to read out ten words, one at a time. Each word will be one of the **o** /u/ words that they have been learning. Tell the children that you will say the word, and then you will read out a sentence containing the word to help them remember what it means. You will then repeat the word on its own again before pausing so that the children can write the word down. For example: **honey**. **Honey** is made by bees. **honey**

1. **honey**. **Honey** is made by bees. **honey**
2. **glove**. I have lost my **glove**. **glove**
3. **love**. I **love** orange juice. **love**
4. **son**. My dad's **son** is my brother. **son**
5. **mother**. My **mother** is great at reading stories. **mother**
6. **brother**. My **brother** likes to listen to music. **brother**
7. **other**. My jumper was dirty so I put the **other** one on. **other**
8. **nothing**. We ate **nothing** until lunchtime. **nothing**
9. **Monday**. On **Monday** I have a spelling test. **Monday**
10. **oven**. We cooked potatoes in the **oven**. **oven**

For those students who need a little more of a spelling challenge, read out the further 'Quiet Zone' words to spell: **dozen**, **another**, **cover**, **above**

Full details of how to carry out assessment can be found on pages 6 and 102 of this guide.

STATION - WEEK 19

Donkey Valley

OBJECTIVES
ey /ee/ sound
Spell and use words containing ey /ee/

Review previous learning

Ask the children if they can recall the spelling content and any examples from the previous spelling lesson. Elicit ideas and remind the children that: The /u/ sound is sometimes spelt as **o**, for example, **honey** and **mother**.

Introducing the rule

Explain to the children that in today's lesson they will learn about words that are spelt with **ey** for the /ee/ sound.

The /ee/ sound can be spelt **ey** at the end of some words. The plural of these words is formed by adding an –**s**, for example, **donkeys** and **monkeys**.

Optional: Review the Letterland story

Talk about the Letterland story to help children remember the spelling pattern (see page 115).

Pupil Book Activity 1: Crossword

1. Draw children's attention to the Word Bank at the top of page 38. Explain that all of these words contain the spelling pattern **ey** for the /ee/ sound at the end of words.
2. Ask the children to read through the words in the Word Bank and talk to a partner about what they mean. Then ask the children if there are any words they are unsure of and explain the meanings to them, looking in the dictionary for a definition if necessary.
3. Ask the children to read each clue, then find the answer words in the Word Bank and write them in the spaces provided.

Answers: a) money; b) key; c) donkey; d) hockey; e) jockey

Pupil Book Activity 2: Write it

1. Model the activity by showing the children how to think of, say and write a sentence using a word from the Word Bank, for example, **donkey**. Write your sentence on the board to show correct punctuation and handwriting formation. For example, say: What is a **donkey**? An animal, similar to a horse, often a grey colour, that brays. So my sentence could be 'I saw a donkey eating grass in the field.'
2. Ask the children to write a sentence for two words from the Word Bank. If children need some support, they could work in pairs to decide on a sentence and say it outloud before writing it. If children need full support, use these example answers to provide a dictated sentence (the adult reads the sentence and the children write it).

Example answers:

a) donkey: I saw a donkey eating grass in the field.

b) valley: We moved to a new house in a valley.

c) alley: I rode my bike down the alley to my friend's house.

d) trolley: I pushed the trolley at the supermarket.

e) chimney: Smoke came out of the chimney on the house.

Pupil Book Activity 3: Choose a ditty

1. Ask the children to carefully read both ditties. Explain that when we want to remember how words are spelt, a useful method is to group them together into a fun ditty or phrase. When you think of one of the words in the ditty, you will automatically remember the other words that went with it.
2. The children could work independently or in pairs. Ask them to choose their favourite ditty and read it lots of times to try and learn it by heart. Challenge them to sing it to any simple melody.
3. Ask children to perform their ditty to the class by reciting or singing it.
4. As an extension to the task, you could also ask the children to find and underline the spelling patterns in the ditties, or draw a picture to illustrate one of them.

Ditties in this lesson:

The monkey played hockey in the alley with the turkey.

A jockey went on a journey with money and a key in a trolley.

Pupil Book Activity 4: Picture match

1. Remind the children of the Word Bank at the top of page 38.
2. Ask the children to find and copy words from the Word Bank to match the pictures.

Answers: a) monkey; b) turkey; c) key; d) trolley

Pupil Book Activity 5: Complete the passage

1. Read the passage to the children, pausing as you reach each gap. Complete the first gap with the children by re-reading to that point and then say: Look at the Word Bank. Which word is somebody you might meet on a train? Elicit children's ideas and establish that the word is **jockey**.
2. Ask the children to fill in the gaps in the rest of the passage independently or with a partner.

Answers: Mum and Jack met a **jockey** on the train to Donkey Valley. He said he was on a **journey** to the **valley** to watch a game of **hockey**. He had a red **trolley** with a **monkey** sticker on the front. He wore a strange silver **key** on a chain around his neck.

Pupil Book Activity 6: Word search

1. Draw the children's attention to the word search at the bottom of page 39. Set the children the challenge of finding 6 **ey** words in the word search. The words may be found horizontally from left to right or vertically from top to bottom.
2. Tell the children to circle each word as they find it and then write the words in the column.

Answers:

d	p	u	l	l	e	y
k	i	d	n	e	y	c
h	o	c	k	e	y	s
e	b	a	l	l	e	y
c	h	i	m	n	e	y
a	d	o	n	k	e	y

ey	
pulley	alley
kidney	chimney
hockey	donkey

Assessment: ey /ee/

Tell the children that you are going to read out ten words, one at a time. Each word will be one of the **ey** /ee/ words that they have been learning. Tell the children that you will say the word, and then you will read out a sentence containing the word to help them remember what it means. You will then repeat the word on its own again before pausing so that the children can write the word down. For example: **donkey**. We went to a farm and saw a **donkey**. **donkey**

1. **donkey**. We went to a farm and saw a **donkey**. **donkey**
2. **valley**. The sides of the **valley** were steep. **valley**
3. **monkey**. The **monkey** swung from branch to branch. **monkey**
4. **money**. I have been saving my **money**. **money**
5. **key**. We found an old iron **key**. **key**
6. **chimney**. Lots of soot fell from the **chimney**. **chimney**
7. **turkey**. The **turkey** pecked at the seeds. **turkey**
8. **hockey**. We watched a **hockey** match. **hockey**
9. **jockey**. The **jockey** rode his horse along the track. **jockey**
10. **trolley**. We filled our **trolley** with food. **trolley**

For those students who need a little more of a spelling challenge, read out the further 'Quiet Zone' words to spell: **journey**, **alley**, **kidney**, **pulley**

Full details of how to carry out assessment can be found on pages 6 and 102 of this guide.

STATION - WEEK 20

Quality Watches

OBJECTIVES

a /o/

Spell and use words containing a /o/ after qu and w.

Review previous learning

Ask the children if they can recall the spelling content and any examples from the previous spelling lesson. Elicit ideas and remind the children that: The /ee/ sound can be spelt **ey** at the end of some words. The plural of these words is formed by adding an **–s**, for example, **donkeys** and **monkeys**.

Introducing the rule

Explain to the children that in today's lesson they will learn about words that are spelt with an **a** for the /o/ sound.

The /o/ sound is most commonly spelt **a** after **qu** and **w**, for example, **quality** and **watch**. The spelling patterns are therefore **qua** and **wa**.

Pupil Book Activity 1: Sort it

1. Draw children's attention to the Word Bank at the top of page 40. Explain that all of these words contain the spelling patterns **qua** and **wa**.
2. Ask the children to read through the words in the Word Bank and talk to a partner about what they mean. Then ask the children if there are any words they are unsure of and explain the meanings to them, looking in the dictionary for a definition if necessary.
3. Ask the children to sort and write each word into the correct box according to the spelling pattern it contains.

Answers:

qua	wa
quantity	watch
squat	want
qualified	wasp
quality	wash
quarrel	swan
squash	wallet
	swallow
	swamp

Pupil Book Activity 2: Crossword

1. Model the activity by reading the first clue aloud twice and then look through the Word Bank to find the correct answer.
2. Ask the children to read each clue, then find the answer words in the Word Bank and write them in the spaces provided.
3. Then ask the children to copy their answers into the correct places on the crossword. Explain that this is a way of checking if they have solved the clues correctly. The answers should fit into the crossword.

Answers: a) swan; b) watch; c) wasp; d) wallet; e) quarrel

Pupil Book Activity 3: Choose a ditty

1. Ask the children to carefully read both ditties. Explain that when we want to remember how words are spelt, a useful method is to group them together into a fun ditty or phrase. When you think of one of the words in the ditty, you will automatically remember the other words that went with it.
2. The children could work independently or in pairs. Ask them to choose their favourite ditty and read it lots of times to try and learn it by heart. Challenge them to sing it to any simple melody.
3. Ask children to perform their ditty to the class by reciting or singing it.
4. As an extension to the task, you could also ask the children to find and underline the spelling patterns in the ditties, or draw a picture to illustrate one of them.

Ditties in this lesson:

The swan went into the swamp for a wash.

The men quarrelled over the quality of the watches.

Pupil Book Activity 4: Picture match

1. Remind the children of the Word Bank at the top of page 40.
2. Ask the children to find and copy words from the Word Bank to match the pictures.

Answers: a) swan; b) watch; c) wasp; d) wallet

Pupil Book Activity 5: Anagrams

1. Draw the children's attention to the anagrams in Activity 5. Explain to the children that the words have been taken from the Word Bank and the letters have been jumbled up into the wrong order.
2. Ask them to look carefully at the jumbled letters and try to work out which words from the Word Bank they are, then correctly write them in the space provided. Remind the children of the spelling patterns as a clue to help them: the letters **qua** and **wa** will be together.
3. As a method of self-checking, encourage the children to count how many letters are in the jumbled word and how many letters they have written in the correct spelling of the word to check that they are the same. If they aren't, suggest to the children that they check their spelling of the word.

Answers: a) want; b) squat; c) squash; d) swallow; e) qualified

Pupil Book Activity 6: Write a story

1. Set the children the challenge of writing their own short story using **qua** and **wa** words. Explain to the children that using the words in this way will help them to remember the words more effectively. Encourage the children to include as many of the Word Bank words as possible.
2. Use the following text as a model to show the children how to write the short story or, alternatively, use the text as a passage dictation by reading each sentence slowly and clearly for the children to write down:

Two men were quarrelling on the train over whether one of them should squash a wasp with his wallet. They were soon distracted by a funny sight through the window. A swan and a swallow were both trying to wash in a swamp!

Assessment: qua, wa /o/

Tell the children that you are going to read out ten words, one at a time. Each word will be one of the **qua** or **wa** /o/ words that they have been learning. Tell the children that you will say the word, and then you will read out a sentence containing the word to help them remember what it means. You will then repeat the word on its own again before pausing so that the children can write the word down. For example: **watch**. I wear my **watch** on my wrist. **watch**

1. **watch**. I wear my **watch** on my wrist. **watch**
2. **wasp**. A **wasp** flew into our kitchen. **wasp**
3. **want**. I **want** to read my book. **want**
4. **swan**. A beautiful **swan** swam across the lake. **swan**
5. **wash**. I **wash** my hands before eating. **wash**
6. **quantity**. Nan has a large **quantity** of cookies. **quantity**
7. **squash**. I pressed the dough to **squash** it. **squash**
8. **squat**. You can **squat** to hide behind the chair. **squat**
9. **qualified**. Miss Hart is **qualified** to be a teacher. **qualified**
10. **quality**. The **quality** is how good something is. **quality**

For those students who need a little more of a spelling challenge, read out the further 'Quiet Zone' words to spell: **wander, wallet**, **swamp**, **quarrel**, **swallow**

Full details of how to carry out assessment can be found on pages 6 and 102 of this guide.

STATION - WEEK 21

Warm Workshop

OBJECTIVES
ar /or/ and **or** /er/

Spell and use words containing ar /or/ and or /er/.

Review previous learning

Ask the children if they can recall the spelling content and any examples from the previous spelling lesson. Elicit ideas and remind the children that: The /o/ sound is most commonly spelt **a** after **qu** and **w**, for example, **quality** and **watch**. The spelling patterns are therefore **qua** and **wa**.

Introducing the rule

Explain to the children that in today's lesson they will learn about words that are spelt with **war** when **ar** sounds like /or/ and **wor** when **or** sounds like /er/. The spelling patterns therefore are **war** and **wor**. There are not many of these words.

Pupil Book Activity 1: Sort it

1. Draw children's attention to the Word Bank at the top of page 42. Explain that all of these words contain the spelling patterns **war** and **wor**.
2. Ask the children to read through the words in the Word Bank and talk to a partner about what they mean. Then ask the children if there are any words they are unsure of and explain the meanings to them, looking in the dictionary for a definition if necessary.
3. Ask the children to sort and write each word into the correct box according to the spelling pattern it contains.

Answers:

war		wor	
warm	wardrobe	world	work
warn	towards	word	worst
swarm	war	worm	worth
reward	dwarf		

Pupil Book Activity 2: Write it

1. Model the activity by showing the children how to think of, say and write a sentence using a word from one of the word boxes in Activity 1, for example, **warm**. Write your sentence on the board to show correct punctuation and handwriting formation. For example, say: What does **warm** mean? It's a temperature, it's not quite hot but it's not cold. So my sentence could be 'I put my socks on to keep my feet warm.'
2. Ask the children to write a sentence for two words from each of the word boxes in Activity 1. If children need some support, they could work in pairs to decide on a sentence and say it outloud before writing it. If children need full support, use these example answers to provide a dictated sentence (the adult reads the sentence and the children write it).

Example answers:

a) warm: I put my socks on to keep my feet warm.

b) swarm: A swarm of bees flew through the forest.

c) reward: I earned a reward for doing my best.

d) worm: I saw a wriggly worm in the garden.

e) work: Mum was asked to work a night-shift.

Pupil Book Activity 3: Choose a ditty

1. Ask the children to carefully read both ditties. Explain that when we want to remember how words are spelt, a useful method is to group them together into a fun ditty or phrase. When you think of one of the words in the ditty, you will automatically remember the other words that went with it.
2. The children could work independently or in pairs. Ask them to choose their favourite ditty and read it lots of times to try and learn it by heart. Challenge them to sing it to any simple melody.
3. Ask children to perform their ditty to the class by reciting or singing it.
4. As an extension to the task, you could also ask the children to find and underline the spelling patterns in the ditties, or draw a picture to illustrate one of them.

Ditties in this lesson:

Warning! It's warm, and swarms of locusts are coming towards us!

The worm had to work hard in the worst soil in the world.

Pupil Book Activity 4: Picture match

1. Remind the children of the Word Bank at the top of page 42.
2. Ask the children to find and copy words from the Word Bank to match the pictures.

Answers: a) worm; b) world; c) swarm; d) reward

Pupil Book Activity 5: Complete the passage

1. Read the passage to the children, pausing as you reach each gap. Complete the first gap with the children by re-reading to that point and then say: Look at the Word Bank. Which word is something that would describe how a day could be? Elicit children's ideas and establish that the word is **warm**.
2. Ask the children to fill in the gaps in the rest of the passage independently or with a partner.

Answers: Billy and his dad were on the train on a very **warm** day. Billy's dad was doing work on a laptop. Billy was reading a book about a magical **wardrobe**. When the children went inside it they went to another **world**. As the train pulled up at the station Billy saw a **swarm** of bees fly past the window. He wanted to **warn** all the other people to watch out. He told the ticket man about the bees, so he could tell the whole train. Billy's dad said that he had been very thoughtful and deserved a **reward**.

Pupil Book Activity 6: Word search

1. Draw the children's attention to the word search at the bottom of page 43. Set the children the challenge of finding 6 **war** and **wor** words in the word search. The words may be found horizontally from left to right or vertically from top to bottom.
2. Tell the children to circle each word as they find it and then write the words in the correct column.

Answers:

w	o	r	k	b	e
a	j	h	w	a	r
f	w	o	r	t	h
i	d	w	a	r	n
s	w	a	r	m	c
w	o	r	l	d	g

war	wor
war	work
warn	worth
swarm	world

Assessment: **war** /or/, **wor** /er/

Tell the children that you are going to read out ten words, one at a time. Each word will be one of the **war** /or/ or **wor** /er/ words that they have been learning. Tell the children that you will say the word, and then you will read out a sentence containing the word to help them remember what it means. You will then repeat the word on its own again before pausing so that the children can write the word down. For example: **world**. I would like to travel around the **world**. **world**

1. **world**. I would like to travel around the **world**. **world**
2. **word**. I find the **word** 'palace' hard to spell. **word**
3. **worm**. I watched a **worm** in the garden. **worm**
4. **work**. My **work** is interesting. **work**
5. **worst**. We had the **worst** weather today. **worst**
6. **warm**. My bath water is **warm**. **warm**
7. **warn**. The bell will ring to **warn** you. **warn**
8. **swarm**. We heard the **swarm** coming. **swarm**
9. **reward**. We earned a class **reward**. **reward**
10. **towards**. The train headed **towards** the tunnel. **towards**

For those students who need a little more of a spelling challenge, read out the further 'Quiet Zone' words to spell: **wardrobe, war, dwarf, worth**

Full details of how to carry out assessment can be found on pages 6 and 102 of this guide.

STATION - WEEK 22

Treasure Measure

OBJECTIVES
S /zh/

Spell and use words containing s /zh/.

Review previous learning

Ask the children if they can recall the spelling content and any examples from the previous spelling lesson. Elicit ideas and remind the children that: The /or/ sound can be spelt as **ar** after **w** and the /er/ sound can be spelt **or** after **w**. The spelling patterns therefore are **war** and **wor**, as in **warm workshop**. There are not many of these words.

Introducing the rule

Explain to the children that in today's lesson they will learn about words that are spelt with **s** for the /zh/ sound. The /zh/ sound can be spelt **s**, for example, **treasure**.

Pupil Book Activity 1: Write it

1. Draw children's attention to the Word Bank at the top of page 44. Explain that all of these words contain the spelling pattern **s** for the /zh/ sound.
2. Ask the children to read through the words in the Word Bank and talk to a partner about what they mean. Then ask the children if there are any words they are unsure of and explain the meanings to them, looking in the dictionary for a definition if necessary.
3. Model the activity by showing the children how to think of, say and write a sentence using the first word, **treasure**. Write your sentence on the board to show correct punctuation and handwriting formation. For example, say: What is **treasure**? It is something that is valuable to someone. It could be a chest of gold but it could also be a family photograph. So my sentence could be 'The children found the treasure.'
4. Ask the children to write a sentence for each of the given words. If children need some support, they could work in pairs to decide on a sentence and say it outloud before writing it. If children need full support, use these example answers to provide a dictated sentence (the adult reads the sentence and the children write it).

Example answers:

a) treasure: The children found the treasure.

b) explosion: We all heard a loud explosion.

c) conclusion: We wrote a conclusion.

d) occasion: The party was a great occasion.

Pupil Book Activity 2: Crossword

1. Model the activity by reading the first clue aloud twice and then look through the Word Bank to find the correct answer.
2. Ask the children to read each clue, then find the answer words in the Word Bank and write them in the spaces provided.
3. Then ask the children to copy their answers into the correct places on the crossword. Explain that this is a way of checking if they have solved the clues correctly. The answers should fit into the crossword.

Answers: a) extension; b) confusion; c) discussion; d) division; e) television

Pupil Book Activity 3: Choose a ditty

1. Ask the children to carefully read both ditties. Explain that when we want to remember how words are spelt, a useful method is to group them together into a fun ditty or phrase. When you think of one of the words in the ditty, you will automatically remember the other words that went with it.
2. The children could work independently or in pairs. Ask them to choose their favourite ditty and read it lots of times to try and learn it by heart. Challenge them to sing it to any simple melody.
3. Ask children to perform their ditty to the class by reciting or singing it.
4. As an extension to the task, you could also ask the children to find and underline the spelling patterns in the ditties, or draw a picture to illustrate one of them.

Ditties in this lesson:

The treasure brought pleasure that you could measure.

The explosion on the television led to confusion and discussion.

Pupil Book Activity 4: Picture match

1. Remind the children of the Word Bank at the top of page 44.
2. Ask the children to find and copy words from the Word Bank to match the pictures.

Answers: a) television; b) treasure; c) measure; d) division

Pupil Book Activity 5: Anagrams

3. Draw the children's attention to the anagrams in Activity 5. Explain to the children that the words have been taken from the Word Bank and the letters have been jumbled up into the wrong order.
4. Ask them to look carefully at the jumbled letters and try to work out which words from the Word Bank they are, then correctly write them in the space provided. Remind the children of the spelling patterns as a clue to help them: the letter **s** has a /zh/ sound.
5. As a method of self-checking, encourage the children to count how many letters are in the jumbled word and how many letters they have written in the correct spelling of the word to check that they are the same. If they aren't, suggest to the children that they check their spelling of the word.

Answers: a) usual; b) explosion; c) revision; d) invasion; e) discussion

Pupil Book Activity 6: Write a story

1. Set the children the challenge of writing their own short story using **s** /zh/ words. Explain to the children that using the words in this way will help them to remember the words more effectively. Encourage the children to include as many of the Word Bank words as possible.
2. Use the following text as a model to show the children how to write the short story or, alternatively, use the text as a passage dictation by reading each sentence slowly and clearly for the children to write down:

Robert was excited to get home. He wanted to watch a television show about an invasion. In the last episode there had been a great explosion. The main character was hunting for treasure. Robert had a discussion about the show with another passenger on the train. He said that the show was a pleasure to watch because there was never any confusion.

Did you know?

1. Tell the children that there are other less common ways to spell the /zh/ sound. These include **g** as in **courgette** and **ge** as in **collage**.

Assessment: s /zh/

Tell the children that you are going to read out twelve words, one at a time. Each word will be one of the **s** /zh/ words that they have been learning. Tell the children that you will say the word, and then you will read out a sentence containing the word to help them remember what it means. You will then repeat the word on its own again before pausing so that the children can write the word down. For example: **measure**. I use a ruler to **measure**. **measure**

1. **measure**. I use a ruler to **measure**. **measure**
2. **pleasure**. It was a **pleasure** to walk in the sunshine. **pleasure**
3. **treasure**. The pirates found a chest of **treasure**. **treasure**
4. **television**. We like to watch **television** after school. **television**
5. **usual**. Mr Green had his **usual** cup of coffee. **usual**
6. **discussion**. The teachers had a **discussion**. **discussion**
7. **division**. **Division** sums are about sharing. **division**
8. **confusion**. The noise led to **confusion**. **confusion**
9. **extension**. My parents are building an **extension**. **extension**
10. **explosion**. There was an **explosion** in the science lab. **explosion**
11. **conclusion**. We all agreed about the **conclusion**. **conclusion**
12. **invasion**. It was like an ant **invasion**. **invasion**

For those students who need a little more of a spelling challenge, read out the six further 'Quiet Zone' words to spell: **possession**, **expression**, **revision**, **progression**, **collusion**, **occasion**

Full details of how to carry out assessment can be found on pages 6 and 102 of this guide.

STATION - WEEK 23
Lovely Refreshment

OBJECTIVES
–ly and –ment

Spell and use words containing –ly and –ment.

Review previous learning

Ask the children if they can recall the spelling content and any examples from the previous spelling lesson. Elicit ideas and remind the children that: The /zh/ sound can be spelt **s**, for example, **treasure**.

Introducing the rule

Explain to the children that in today's lesson they will learn about words that are spelt with the endings (suffixes) –**ly** and –**ment**.

If a suffix starts with a consonant letter, it is added straight on to most root words without any change to the last letter of those words, for example, **lovely** = love + ly and **excitement** = excite + ment.

> **Optional: Review the Letterland Grammar analogies**
>
> Learn the analogy to help children understand suffixes (see page 118).

Pupil Book Activity 1: Sort it

1. Draw children's attention to the Word Bank at the top of page 46. Explain that all of these words contain the spelling patterns –**ly** and –**ment**.
2. Ask the children to read through the words in the Word Bank and talk to a partner about what they mean. Then ask the children if there are any words they are unsure of and explain the meanings to them, looking in the dictionary for a definition if necessary.
3. Ask the children to sort and write each word into the correct box according to the spelling pattern.

Answers:

–ly		–ment	
lovely	quickly	excitement	movement
badly	softly	refreshment	agreement
safely	loudly	enjoyment	pavement
happily	lonely		amazement
slowly		payment	improvement

Pupil Book Activity 2: Write it

1. Model the activity by showing the children how to think of, say and write a sentence using a word from one of the word boxes in Activity 1, for example, **lovely**. Write your sentence on the board to show correct punctuation and handwriting formation. For example, say: What does **lovely** mean? It describes someone or something that is particularly nice or pleasant. So my sentence could be 'My teacher is always lovely.'
2. Ask the children to write a sentence for two words from each of the boxes in Activity 2. If children need some support, they could work in pairs to decide on a sentence and say it outloud before writing it. If children need full support, use these example answers to provide a dictated sentence (the adult reads the sentence and the children write it).

Example answers:

a) lovely: My teacher is always lovely.

b) badly: I wanted the new toy so badly.

c) *safely: Always look twice to cross the road safely.*

d) *excitement: I could not contain my excitement.*

e) *refreshment: At half time we needed a refreshment.*

Pupil Book Activity 3: Choose a ditty

1. Ask the children to carefully read both ditties. Explain that when we want to remember how words are spelt, a useful method is to group them together into a fun ditty or phrase. When you think of one of the words in the ditty, you will automatically remember the other words that went with it.
2. The children could work independently or in pairs. Ask them to choose their favourite ditty and read it lots of times to try and learn it by heart. Challenge them to sing it to any simple melody.
3. Ask children to perform their ditty to the class by reciting or singing it.
4. As an extension to the task, you could also ask the children to find and underline the spelling patterns in the ditties, or draw a picture to illustrate one of them.

Ditties in this lesson:

We were full of excitement about the lovely refreshments.

We slowly and safely made funny movements along the pavement.

Pupil Book Activity 4: Picture match

1. Remind the children of the Word Bank at the top of page 46.
2. Ask the children to find and copy words from the Word Bank to match the pictures.

Answers: a) refreshment; b) loudly; c) amazement; d) payment

Pupil Book Activity 5: Complete the passage

1. Read the passage to the children, pausing as you reach each gap. Complete the first gap with the children by re-reading to that point and then say: Look at the Word Bank. Which word describes how you can give something? Elicit children's ideas and establish that the word is **slowly**.
2. Ask the children to fill in the gaps in the rest of the passage independently or with a partner.

Answers: Cornelia watched the old man as he **slowly** gave the **payment** for his ticket. He was always on his own so she thought he may be **lonely**. He nodded in **agreement** when the ticket man said that it was getting cold. Cornelia also heard him say that there had been an **improvement** in the train timetable. Then he moved **happily** down to his seat.

Pupil Book Activity 6: Word search

1. Draw the children's attention to the word search at the bottom of page 47. Set the children the challenge of finding 6 –**ly** and –**ment** words in the word search. The words may be found horizontally from left to right or vertically from top to bottom.
2. Tell the children to circle each word as they find it and then write the words in the correct column.

Answers:

m	o	v	e	m	e	n	t
s	o	f	t	l	y	b	e
f	l	b	a	d	l	y	d
c	p	a	y	m	e	n	t
a	q	u	i	c	k	l	y
p	a	v	e	m	e	n	t

–ly	–ment
softly	movement
badly	payment
quickly	pavement

Did you know?

Tell the children that the exception to the rules are a) the word **argument** which loses its end **e** when **ment** is added, for example, **argue** + **ment** = **argument** and b) root words ending in **–y** with a consonant before it but only if the root word has more than one syllable, for example, **merriment** (**merry** + **ment** = **merriment**).

Assessment: –ly, –ment

Tell the children that you are going to read out twelve words, one at a time. Each word will be one of the **–ly** or **–ment** words that they have been learning. Tell the children that you will say the word, and then you will read out a sentence containing the word to help them remember what it means. You will then repeat the word on its own again before pausing so that the children can write the word down. For example: **badly**. I want the new toy so **badly**. **badly**

1. **badly**. I want the new toy so **badly**. **badly**
2. **happily**. We skipped **happily** down the road. **happily**
3. **slowly**. My tortoise walks **slowly**. **slowly**
4. **quickly**. My hamster runs **quickly**. **quickly**
5. **softly**. My mum sings **softly** to us at bedtime. **softly**
6. **loudly**. My sister **loudly** bangs her drum kit. **loudly**
7. **refreshment**. The orange wedges provide great **refreshment**. **refreshment**
8. **enjoyment**. The music brings **enjoyment** to us all. **enjoyment**
9. **payment**. We gave **payment** for the tickets. **payment**
10. **movement**. I heard a **movement** in the middle of the night. **movement**
11. **pavement**. The construction workers laid a new **pavement**. **pavement**
12. **lovely**. The spring flowers are **lovely**. **lovely**

For those students who need a little more of a spelling challenge, read out the further 'Quiet Zone' words to spell: **safely**, **lonely**, **amazement**, **excitement**, **agreement**

Full details of how to carry out assessment can be found on pages 6 and 102 of this guide.

STATION - WEEK 24

Care*ful*! Dark*ness*!

OBJECTIVES
–ful, –less and –ness

Spell and use words containing suffixes –ful and –less and –ness.

Review previous learning

Ask the children if they can recall the spelling content and any examples from the previous spelling lesson. Elicit ideas and remind the children that they were learning about the endings (suffixes) –**ly** and –**ment**. If a suffix starts with a consonant letter, it is added straight on to most root words without any change to the last letter of those words, for example, **lovely** = **love** + **ly** and **excitement** = **excite** + **ment**.

Introducing the rule

Explain to the children that in today's lesson they will learn about words that are spelt with endings (suffixes) –**ful**, –**less** and –**ness**.

If a suffix starts with a consonant letter, it is added straight on to most root words without any change to the last letter of those words.

Optional: Review the Letterland story

To help, you might like to talk about Giant Full, who lives in Letterland (see page 115).

Optional: Review the Letterland Grammar analogies

Learn the analogy to help children understand suffixes (see page 118).

Pupil Book Activity 1: Sort it

1. Draw children's attention to the Word Bank at the top of page 48. Explain that all of these words contain the spelling patterns –**ful**, –**less** and –**ness**.
2. Ask the children to read through the words in the Word Bank and talk to a partner about what they mean. Then ask the children if there are any words they are unsure of and explain the meanings to them, looking in the dictionary for a definition if necessary.
3. Ask the children to sort and write each word into the correct box according to the spelling pattern it contains.

Answers:

–ful	–less	–ness
careful	hopeless	sadness
playful	plainness	
helpful	darkness	fairness
forgetful	careless	
tearful	thoughtless	kindness
	useless	
cheerful	fearless	foolishness
	effortless	

Pupil Book Activity 2: Crossword

1. Model the activity by reading the first clue aloud twice and then look through the Word Bank to find the correct answer.
2. Ask the children to read each clue, then find the answer words in the Word Bank and write them in the spaces provided.
3. Then ask the children to copy their answers into the correct places on the crossword. Explain that this is a way of checking if they have solved the clues correctly. The answers should fit into the crossword.

Answers: a) forgetful; b) playful; c) fearless; d) helpful; e) careful

Pupil Book Activity 3: Choose a ditty

1. Ask the children to carefully read both ditties. Explain that when we want to remember how words are spelt, a useful method is to group them together into a fun ditty or phrase. When you think of one of the words in the ditty, you will automatically remember the other words that went with it.
2. The children could work independently or in pairs. Ask them to choose their favourite ditty and read it lots of times to try and learn it by heart. Challenge them to sing it to any simple melody.
3. Ask children to perform their ditty to the class by reciting or singing it.
4. As an extension to the task, you could also ask the children to find and underline the spelling patterns in the ditties, or draw a picture to illustrate one of them.

Ditties in this lesson:

Be fearless but careful in the darkness.

Show fairness and kindness, be helpful and cheerful.

Pupil Book Activity 4: Picture match

1. Remind the children of the Word Bank at the top of page 48.
2. Ask the children to find and copy words from the Word Bank to match the pictures.

Answers: a) forgetful; b) helpful; c) playful; d) darkness

Pupil Book Activity 5: Anagrams

1. Draw the children's attention to the anagrams in Activity 5. Explain to the children that the words have been taken from the Word Bank and the letters have been jumbled up into the wrong order.
2. Ask them to look carefully at the jumbled letters and try to work out which words from the Word Bank they are, then correctly write them in the space provided. Remind the children of the spelling patterns as a clue to help them: the words end in the suffixes **-ful**, **-less** and **-ness**.
3. As a method of self-checking, encourage the children to count how many letters are in the jumbled word and how many letters they have written in the correct spelling of the word to check that they are the same. If they aren't, suggest to the children that they check their spelling of the word.

Answers: a) kindness; b) tearful; c) plainness; d) useless; e) hopeless

Pupil Book Activity 6: Write a story

1. Set the children the challenge of writing their own short story using **-ful**, **-less** and **-ness** words. Explain to the children that using the words in this way will help them to remember the words more

effectively. Encourage the children to include as many of the Word Bank words as possible.

2. Use the following text as a model to show the children how to write the short story or, alternatively, use the text as a passage dictation by reading each sentence slowly and clearly for the children to write down:

As the train went through a long tunnel, it was suddenly plunged into darkness. Linda felt tearful and worried. Then a stranger showed her great kindness. She came to sit next to her and introduced her playful puppy. Playing with the little puppy was effortless. Soon Linda felt cheerful.

Assessment: –ful, –less, –ness

Tell the children that you are going to read out twelve words, one at a time. Each word will be one of the –ful, –less or –ness words that they have been learning. Tell the children that you will say the word, and then you will read out a sentence containing the word to help them remember what it means. You will then repeat the word on its own again before pausing so that the children can write the word down. For example: **careful**. I am **careful** when I carry my drink. **careful**

1. **careful**. I am **careful** when I carry my drink. **careful**
2. **playful**. My brother and I felt **playful**. **playful**
3. **helpful**. I always try to be **helpful**. **helpful**
4. **tearful**. The sad film made Mum **tearful**. **tearful**
5. **careless**. People who drop litter are **careless**. **careless**
6. **useless**. A bucket with a hole in the bottom is **useless**. **useless**
7. **fearless**. I am **fearless** at the fairground. **fearless**
8. **hopeless**. We felt **hopeless** during the flood. **hopeless**
9. **sadness**. There was a feeling of **sadness** amongst us. **sadness**
10. **darkness**. I love the **darkness**. **darkness**
11. **fairness**. I like to see honesty and **fairness** in people. **fairness**
12. **kindness**. The most important quality to have is **kindness**. **kindness**

For those students who need a little more of a spelling challenge, read out the six further 'Quiet Zone' words to spell: **forgetful**, **cheerful**, **effortless**, **thoughtless**, **plainness**, **foolishness**

Full details of how to carry out assessment can be found on pages 6 and 102 of this guide.

STATION - WEEK 25
Don't Run!

OBJECTIVES
Contractions
Spell and use words containing apostrophes for contractions.

Review previous learning
Ask the children if they can recall the spelling content and any examples from the previous spelling lesson. Elicit ideas and remind the children that: They were learning about words that are spelt with endings (suffixes) –**ful**, –**less** and –**ness**.

If a suffix starts with a consonant letter, it is added straight on to most root words without any change to the last letter of those words.

Introducing the rule
Explain to the children that in today's lesson they will learn about words called **contractions**. A contraction is when two words are put together and shortened to make a more informal version of the words, for example, **they** + **have** = **they've**. In contractions, the apostrophe shows where a letter or letters would have been if the words had been written in full.

Optional: Review the Letterland Grammar analogies
Learn the analogy to help children understand contractions (see page 118).

Pupil Book Activity 1: Write the words

1. Draw children's attention to the Word Bank at the top of page 50. Explain that all of these words are contractions.
2. Ask the children to read through the words in the Word Bank and talk to a partner about what they mean. Then ask the children if there are any words they are unsure of and explain the meanings to them, looking in the dictionary for a definition if necessary. Talk about the full words for each contraction and if you choose to, expand each contraction to its full words on the board – then choose whether to leave or remove any words from the board before children perform the next part of the activity.
3. Ask the children to look at the example of the full words written to match the contraction in the box. Ask children to write the full words to match all of the contractions shown.

Answers:

don't	can't	didn't	wasn't
do not	can not	did not	was not
he'd	they've	we're	hasn't
he had / would	they have	we are	has not
couldn't	shouldn't	haven't	I've
could not	should not	have not	I have

Pupil Book Activity 2: Write it

1. Model the activity by showing the children how to think of, say and write a sentence using a word from the Word Bank, for example, **don't**. Write your sentence on the board to show correct punctuation and handwriting formation. For example, say: What does **don't** mean? It means **do not**. So my sentence could be 'Don't stand on the sofa.'
2. Ask the children to write a sentence for two words selected from the Word Bank. If children need

some support, they could work in pairs to decide on a sentence and say it outloud before writing it. If children need full support, use these example answers to provide a dictated sentence (the adult reads the sentence and the children write it).

Example answers:

a) don't: Don't stand on the sofa.

b) can't: We can't go to the library today.

c) didn't: I didn't pack my sports kit.

d) wasn't: It wasn't my fault that we lost the match.

e) he'd: Albert said he'd finished the book.

Pupil Book Activity 3: Choose a ditty

1. Ask the children to carefully read both ditties. Explain that when we want to remember how words are spelt, a useful method is to group them together into a fun ditty or phrase. When you think of one of the words in the ditty, you will automatically remember the other words that went with it.
2. The children could work independently or in pairs. Ask them to choose their favourite ditty and read it lots of times to try and learn it by heart. Challenge them to sing it to any simple melody.
3. Ask children to perform their ditty to the class by reciting or singing it.
4. As an extension to the task, you could also ask the children to find and underline the spelling patterns in the ditties, or draw a picture to illustrate one of them.

Ditties in this lesson:

I didn't, I can't, I won't watch the television.

We couldn't, we wouldn't, we shouldn't paddle in the stream.

Pupil Book Activity 4: Write the contractions

1. Remind the children of Activity 1 where they expanded the contractions back into their full words.
2. Explain that this time, they will look at the full words and write them as their contractions.
3. Ask the children to remind you and one another of where the apostrophe needs to go (in the place of the letters being removed).
4. Use the example provided to show how the words **do** and **not** have been put together and the apostrophe used to replace the second **o**.
5. Ask children to complete the boxes by writing the contractions.

Answers:

do not	would not	they had	we have
don't	wouldn't	they'd	we've
she had	I have	they are	has not
she'd	I've	they're	hasn't
should not	we are	they have	did not
shouldn't	we're	they've	didn't

Pupil Book Activity 5: Complete the passage

1. Read the passage to the children, pausing as you reach each gap. Complete the first gap with the children by re-reading to that point and then say: Look at the Word Bank. Which word shows that the children were not sitting still? Elicit children's ideas and establish that the word is **wouldn't**.
2. Ask the children to fill in the gaps in the rest of the passage independently or with a partner.

Answers: The children **wouldn't** sit still, and Mother was fed up. She **didn't** want to moan at them, but **she'd** had enough. It **wasn't** long until the train arrived at the station. '**We**'re nearly home,' said Mother cheerily.

Pupil Book Activity 6: Word search

1. Draw the children's attention to the word search at the bottom of page 51. Set the children the challenge of finding 6 contraction words (without their apostrophes) in the word search. The words may be found horizontally from left to right or vertically from top to bottom.
2. Tell the children to circle each word as they find it and then write the words in the correct column – adding the apostrophes in the correct places.

Answers:

d	i	d	n'	t	a	h
k	c	o	j	h	e'	d
e	t	h	e	y'	v	e
c	a	n'	t	b	n	f
l	w	o	n'	t	d	i
p	g	m	w	e'	r	e

Contractions	
didn't	can't
he'd	won't
they've	we're

Assessment: Contractions

1. Tell the children that you are going to read out twelve words, one at a time. Each word will be one of the contraction words that they have been learning. Tell the children that you will say the word, and then you will read out a sentence containing the word to help them remember what it means. You will then repeat the word on its own again before pausing so that the children can write the word down. For example: **don't**. I **don't** want to get up early. **don't**

1. **don't**. I **don't** want to get up early. **don't**
2. **can't**. I **can't** wait until Tuesday. **can't**
3. **won't**. I **won't** be the first one to finish. **won't**
4. **I've**. **I've** tidied my room. **I've**
5. **wasn't**. It **wasn't** my book that was found. **wasn't**
6. **he'd**. He said **he'd** see us tomorrow. **he'd**
7. **she'd**. I heard **she'd** gone to a new school. **she'd**
8. **they'd**. If **they'd** left earlier, we would be on time. **they'd**
9. **they've**. **They've** gone for a walk. **they've**
10. **they're**. **They're** such kind people. **they're**
11. **we're**. I think **we're** the first ones here. **we're**
12. **we've**. **We've** got a long way to travel. **we've**

For those students who need a little more of a spelling challenge, read out the six further 'Quiet Zone' words to spell: **hasn't, couldn't, shouldn't, wouldn't, haven't, didn't**

Full details of how to carry out assessment can be found on pages 6 and 102 of this guide.

STATION - WEEK 26

Tom's Ticket

OBJECTIVES
Possessive apostrophes
Spell and use words containing possessive apostrophes.

Review previous learning

Ask the children if they can recall the spelling content and any examples from the previous spelling lesson. Elicit ideas and remind the children that: They were learning about words called contractions. A contraction is when two words are put together and shortened to make a more informal version of the words, for example, **they** + **have** = **they've**. In contractions, the apostrophe shows where a letter or letters would have been if the words had been written in full.

Introducing the rule

Explain to the children that in today's lesson they will learn about another use for apostrophes called **possessive apostrophes**.

An apostrophe is a punctuation mark used to show who owns something. If the word is singular, **'s** is added, even if the word ends in **s**.

Optional: Review the Letterland Grammar analogies

Learn the analogy to help children understand possessive apostrophes (see page 118).

Pupil Book Activity 1: Write the words

1. Draw children's attention to the Word Bank at the top of page 52. Explain that all of these words are showing the use of **possessive apostrophes**.
2. Ask the children to read through the words in the Word Bank and talk to a partner about what they mean. Then ask the children if there are any words they are unsure of and explain the meanings to them, for example, **tree's** means something belonging to the **tree**, like the **tree's leaves**.
3. Ask the children to look at the example in the first box. Ask children to write the words, adding the apostrophe in the correct place each time.

Answers:

Toms socks	Kates ball	Tesss hat	Ravis book
Tom's socks	Kate's ball	Tess's hat	Ravi's book
the girls coat	the childs toy	the mans glasses	the cats paws
the girl's coat	the child's toy	the man's glasses	the cat's paws
the teachers desk	the babys cot	the shops door	the trees leaves
the teacher's desk	the baby's cot	the shop's door	the tree's leaves

Pupil Book Activity 2: Fill the gaps

1. Model the activity by reading the first phrase aloud and then asking, 'Whose rattle is it?'. Elicit ideas and establish that it is the **baby's** rattle. Show how to write **baby's** including placing the **possessive apostrophe** before the **s**.
2. Ask the children to read each phrase, establish who the item belongs to and then write the missing words on the lines. Remind them to include the possessive apostrophes in the correct places.

Answers: a) baby's; b) woman's; c) doctor's; d) dog's; e) man's; f) teacher's

Pupil Book Activity 3: Choose a ditty

1. Ask the children to carefully read both ditties. Explain that when we want to remember how words are spelt, a useful method is to group them together into a fun ditty or phrase. When you think of one of the words in the ditty, you will automatically remember the other words that went with it.
2. The children could work independently or in pairs. Ask them to choose their favourite ditty and read it lots of times to try and learn it by heart. Challenge them to sing it to any simple melody.
3. Ask children to perform their ditty to the class by reciting or singing it.
4. As an extension to the task, you could also ask the children to find and underline the possessive apostrophes in the ditties, or draw a picture to illustrate one of them.

Ditties in this lesson:

Tess's dress and Kate's skates are in Mum's bag.

The tree's leaves blew into the shop's door next to the baby's pram.

Pupil Book Activity 4: Write it

1. Draw children's attention to the picture of the station Lost Property.
2. Ask children to talk with a partner about the items they can see and who each item belongs to.
3. Model how to write a sentence using one of the examples in the picture, for example: These are Kate's flowers.
4. Ask the children to write their own sentences to show who the property belongs to. Remind them that they must include the **possessive apostrophe**.

Example answers: (may vary but accept them if they show the possessive apostrophe)

These are Kate's flowers.

This is Ravi's suitcase.

This is the baby's teddy bear.

These are Tom's shoes.

This is Megan's hat.

These are the man's sunglasses.

Pupil Book Activity 5: Correct it

1. Ask the children to read the three sentences in Activity 5 and ask them to tell you, or a partner, what is missing from the sentences.
2. Ask the children to rewrite the sentences using possessive apostrophes correctly and adding capital letters and full stops where required.

Answers:

a) The train's windows were clean and sparkly.

b) The conductor's ticket machine was broken.

c) The station's lost property desk was full.

Assessment: Possessive apostrophes

Tell the children that you are going to read out ten words, one at a time. Each word will be one of the

possessive apostrophe words that they have been learning. Tell the children that you will say the word, and then you will read out a sentence containing the word to help them remember what it means. You will then repeat the word on its own again before pausing so that the children can write the word down. For example: **Tom's**. This is **Tom's** pen. **Tom's**

1. **Tom's**. This is **Tom's** pen. **Tom's**
2. **Kate's**. That is **Kate's** bag. **Kate's**
3. **Ravi's**. Those are **Ravi's** sweets. **Ravi's**
4. **boy's**. These are the **boy's** shoes. **boy's**
5. **girl's**. That is the **girl's** book. **girl's**
6. **cat's**. Look at the **cat's** toy. **cat's**
7. **dog's**. Look at the **dog's** basket. **dog's**.
8. **man's**. That is the **man's** saxophone. **man's**
9. **shop's**. We enjoyed the **shop's** opening day. **shop's**
10. **baby's**. I heard the **baby's** cries. **baby's**

For those students who need a little more of a spelling challenge, read out the further 'Quiet Zone' words to spell: **woman's**, **doctor's**, **teacher's**, **tree's**, **Tess's**

Full details of how to carry out assessment can be found on pages 6 and 102 of this guide.

STATION - WEEK 27

Action Station

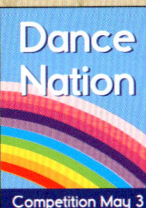

OBJECTIVES
–tion

Spell and use words containing the suffix –tion.

Review previous learning

Ask the children if they can recall the spelling content and any examples from the previous spelling lesson. Elicit ideas and remind the children that: They were learning about another use for apostrophes called **possessive apostrophes**.

A possessive apostrophe is a punctuation mark used to show who owns something. If the word is singular, **'s** is added, even if the word ends in **s**.

Introducing the rule

Explain to the children that in today's lesson they will learn about words that are spelt with the suffix –**tion**.

There are lots of words that have the suffix –**tion**.

Optional: Review the Letterland story

To help, talk about the teacher Mr 'Tion, who lives in Letterland (see page 115)!

Pupil Book Activity 1: Fill the gaps

1. Draw children's attention to the Word Bank at the top of page 54. Explain that all of these words contain the spelling pattern –**tion**.
2. Ask the children to read through the words in the Word Bank and talk to a partner about what they mean. Then ask the children if there are any words they are unsure of and explain the meanings to them, looking in the dictionary for a definition if necessary.
3. Ask the children to read each clue, then find the answer words in the Word Bank and write them in the spaces provided.

Answers: a) lotion; b) station; c) relation; d) fiction; e) introduction

Pupil Book Activity 2: Write it

1. Model the activity by showing the children how to think of, say and write a sentence using the a word from the Word Bank, for example, **station**. Write your sentence on the board to show correct punctuation and handwriting formation. For example, say: What is a **station**? A place, like a train station. So my sentence could be 'The train station is a busy place.'
2. Ask the children to write a sentence for two words from the Word Bank. If children need some support, they could work in pairs to decide on a sentence and say it outloud before writing it. If children need full support, use these example answers to provide a dictated sentence (the adult reads the sentence and the children write it).

Example answers:

a) station: The train station is a busy place.

b) motion: The roller coaster is in constant motion.

c) education: We hope to gain an education.

d) imagination: I love to make up stories with my imagination.

e) competition: I entered a competition.

Pupil Book Activity 3: Choose a ditty

1. Ask the children to carefully read both ditties. Explain that when we want to remember how words are spelt, a useful method is to group them together into a fun ditty or phrase. When you think of one of the words in the ditty, you will automatically remember the other words that went with it.
2. The children could work independently or in pairs. Ask them to choose their favourite ditty and read it lots of times to try and learn it by heart. Challenge them to sing it to any simple melody.
3. Ask children to perform their ditty to the class by reciting or singing it.
4. As an extension to the task, you could also ask the children to find and underline the spelling patterns in the ditties, or draw a picture to illustrate one of them.

Ditties in this lesson:

Did I mention that the education train is in motion at Action Station?

Use your imagination to write a fiction story with a great introduction.

Pupil Book Activity 4: Picture match

1. Remind the children of the Word Bank at the top of page 54.
2. Ask the children to find and copy words from the Word Bank to match the pictures.

Answers: a) fiction; b) station; c) education; d) lotion

Pupil Book Activity 5: Complete the passage

1. Read the passage to the children, pausing as you reach each gap. Complete the first gap with the children by re-reading to that point and then say: Look at the Word Bank. Which word might go together with the word 'master'? Elicit children's ideas and establish that the word is **station**.
2. Ask the children to fill in the gaps in the rest of the passage independently or with a partner.

Answers: The <u>**station**</u> master decided to hold a <u>**competition**</u>. The task was to write a <u>**fiction**</u> story about a plan to reduce the amount of <u>**pollution**</u> created by the <u>**nation**</u>. He made a leaflet that gave an <u>**explanation**</u> of the task that schools could show children. He told them to use their <u>**imagination**</u> when writing the story.

Pupil Book Activity 6: Word search

1. Draw the children's attention to the word search at the bottom of page 55. Set the children the challenge of finding 6 –**tion** words in the word search. The words may be found horizontally from left to right or vertically from top to bottom.
2. Tell the children to circle each word as they find it and then write the words in the correct column.

Answers:

m	o	t	i	o	n	c	g
r	e	l	a	t	i	o	n
f	r	a	c	t	i	o	n
d	n	a	t	i	o	n	d
a	s	e	c	t	i	o	n
m	e	n	t	i	o	n	e

–tion	
motion	nation
relation	section
fraction	mention

Assessment: –tion

Tell the children that you are going to read out twelve words, one at a time. Each word will be one of the –**tion** words that they have been learning. Tell the children that you will say the word, and then you will read out a sentence containing the word to help them remember what it means. You will then repeat the word on its own again before pausing so that the children can write the word down. For example: **action**. Take **action** to get things done. **action**

1. **action**. Take **action** to get things done. **action**
2. **station**. We waited at the **station**. **station**
3. **mention**. Tanya did **mention** that you were here. **mention**
4. **fiction**. My favourite books are **fiction**. **fiction**
5. **motion**. The **motion** of the boat made us queasy. **motion**
6. **section**. This **section** of the shop is for hats. **section**
7. **fraction**. Three quarters is a big **fraction**. **fraction**
8. **lotion**. We put on the sun **lotion**. **lotion**
9. **education**. School gives us an **education**. **education**
10. **pollution**. The cars emitted **pollution**. **pollution**
11. **relation**. A **relation** is a family member. **relation**
12. **competition**. I won the **competition**. **competition**

For those students who need a little more of a spelling challenge, read out the six further 'Quiet Zone' words to spell: **explanation**, **nation**, **completion**, **imagination**, **operation**, **introduction**

Full details of how to carry out assessment can be found on pages 6 and 102 of this guide.

STATION - WEEK 28
Blue Sea (Blew See)

OBJECTIVES
Homophones
Spell and use words that are **homophones** or **near homophones**

Review previous learning
Ask the children if they can recall the spelling content and any examples from the previous spelling lesson. Elicit ideas and remind the children that they were learning about words that are spelt with the suffix **–tion**.

Introducing the rule
Explain to the children that in today's lesson they will learn about words that are **homophones** and **near homophones**.

Some words sound the same as others, but they have different meanings and spellings. They can be easy to confuse so it is important to learn the differences.

Pupil Book Activity 1: Match it
1. Draw children's attention to the Word Bank at the top of page 56. Explain that all of these words are **homophones** or **near homophones**.
2. Ask the children to read through the words in the Word Bank and talk to a partner about what they mean. Then ask the children if there are any words they are unsure of and explain the meanings to them, looking in the dictionary for a definition if necessary.
3. Ask the children to draw lines to match the **homophone** and **near homophone** pairs.

Answers:

night – knight
blue – blew
hear – here
quiet – quite
bear – bare
one – won

Pupil Book Activity 2: Crossword
1. Model the activity by reading the first clue aloud twice and then look through the Word Bank to find the correct answer.
2. Ask the children to read each clue, then find the answer words in the Word Bank and write them in the spaces provided.
3. Then ask the children to copy their answers into the correct places on the crossword. Explain that this is a way of checking if they have solved the clues correctly. The answers should fit into the crossword.

Answers: a) one; b) bear; c) blue; d) night; e) quiet

Pupil Book Activity 3: Choose a ditty
1. Ask the children to carefully read both ditties. Explain that when we want to remember how words are spelt, a useful method is to group them together into a fun ditty or phrase. When you think of one of the words in the ditty, you will automatically remember the other words that went with it.
2. The children could work independently or in pairs. Ask them to choose their favourite ditty and read it lots of times to try and learn it by heart. Challenge them to sing it to any simple melody.
3. Ask children to perform their ditty to the class by reciting or singing it.
4. As an extension to the task, you could also ask the children to find and underline the spelling patterns

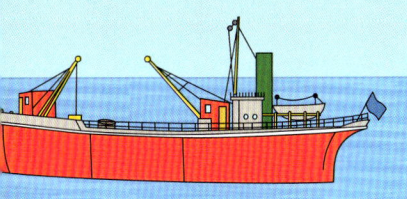

in the ditties, or draw a picture to illustrate one of them.

Ditties in this lesson:

The knight set off at night to see the sea.

The bare bear was quite quiet when he went to catch two fish at the river.

Pupil Book Activity 4: Picture match

1. Remind the children of the Word Bank at the top of page 56.
2. Ask the children to find and copy words from the Word Bank to match the pictures.

Answers: a) knight; b) bear; c) two; d) sun

Pupil Book Activity 5: Anagrams

3. Draw the children's attention to the anagrams in Activity 5. Explain to the children that the words have been taken from the Word Bank and the letters have been jumbled up into the wrong order.
4. Ask them to look carefully at the jumbled letters and try to work out which words from the Word Bank they are, then correctly write them in the space provided.
5. As a method of self-checking, encourage the children to count how many letters are in the jumbled word and how many letters they have written in the correct spelling of the word to check that they are the same. If they aren't, suggest to the children that they check their spelling of the word.

Answers: a) son; b) hear; c) here; d) there; e) their

Pupil Book Activity 6: Write a story

1. Set the children the challenge of writing their own short story using **homophone** and **near homophone** words. Explain to the children that using the words in this way will help them to remember the words more effectively. Encourage the children to include as many of the Word Bank words as possible.
2. Use the following text as a model to show the children how to write the short story or, alternatively, use the text as a passage dictation by reading each sentence slowly and clearly for the children to write down:

The station master blew his blue whistle and the train pulled off from the platform. It was night time and the new train was called the knight flight. It was quite a quiet train. All you could hear was a gentle choo-choo as it left.

Did you know?

There are some words that sound the same and are spelt the same but they have different meanings, for example, **train** (a form of transport) and **train** (to practise a skill). These words are called **homonyms**.

Assessment: Homophones and near homophones

Tell the children that you are going to read out nineteen words, one at a time. Each word will be one of the **homophone** or **near homophone** words that they have been learning. Tell the children that you will say the word, and then you will read out a sentence containing the word to help them remember what it means. You will then repeat the word on its own again before pausing so that the children can write the word down. For example: **blue**. My favourite colour is **blue**. **blue**

1. **blue**. My favourite colour is **blue**. **blue**
2. **blew**. The teacher **blew** the whistle. **blew**
3. **sea**. The boat sailed across the **sea**. **sea**
4. **see**. I can **see** you hiding there. **see**
5. **here**. We are finally **here**. **here**
6. **hear**. I can **hear** an owl hooting. **hear**
7. **bare**. My baby brother was **bare** in the bath. **bare**
8. **bear**. I have a grey teddy **bear**. **bear**
9. **one**. I have **one** pair of trainers. **one**
10. **won**. I **won** the school contest. **won**
11. **sun**. The **sun** is shining brightly. **sun**
12. **son**. My dad's **son** is my brother. **son**
13. **to**. I am happy **to** help you. **to**
14. **too**. It is **too** cold to go outside. **too**
15. **two**. I have **two** ears. **two**
16. **be**. It can't **be** true. **be**
17. **bee**. The **bee** buzzed as it flew. **bee**
18. **night**. It was late at **night**. **night**
19. **knight**. The **knight** rode his steed on an adventure. **knight**

For those students who need a little more of a spelling challenge, read out the further 'Quiet Zone' words to spell: **there**, **they're**, **their**, **quite**, **quiet**

Full details of how to carry out assessment can be found on pages 6 and 102 of this guide.

STATION - WEEK 29

Busy People

OBJECTIVES
Tricky words
Spell and use some common exception words

Review previous learning

Ask the children if they can recall the spelling rule or any example words from the previous spelling lesson. Elicit ideas and remind the children that: They were learning about words that are **homophones** and **near homophones**.

Some words sound the same as others, but they have different meanings and spellings. They can be easy to confuse so it is important to learn the differences.

Introducing the rule

Explain to the children that in today's lesson they will learn about words that can be difficult to spell because the letter-sound correspondences in them have not yet been taught, but the words are so useful that we want to use them now.

Some words do not sound the way you might expect them to. Pay attention to which parts of the word you know and which parts are tricky.

Pupil Book Activity 1: Read the words

1. Draw the children's attention to the Word Bank in the left-hand column of page 58. Explain that all of these words contain parts that have not yet been taught but that it is likely the children will know how to read the words from encountering them in reading books.
2. Ask the children to read through the words in the Word Bank and talk to a partner about what they mean. Then ask the children if there are any words they are unsure of and explain the meanings to them, looking in the dictionary for a definition if necessary.
3. Ask the children to read the example sentences in the second column to help them understand the words in context.

Pupil Book Activity 2: Colour the parts

1. Draw the children's attention to the third column, which contains the words shown so that each phoneme (sound) is distinguishable.
2. Ask the children to say the sounds while thinking carefully about the whole word. Remind them that the letters may not sound the way they expect.
3. Ask the children to colour the easy parts of the word in green and the tricky parts in orange. For example, in the word 'busy' the letter **u** sounds like an /i/ and the letter **s** sounds like /z/. Alternatively ask them to write a wiggly line underneath the tricky part.

Pupil Book Activity 3: Write the words

1. In the final column, ask the children to write each word. If they feel confident, they could cover up the information in the other columns. If they lack confidence, they should copy the spelling from the other columns and say the word as they write it.
2. Remind the children to look back through their spellings to check for accuracy.

Assessment: Tricky Words

Tell the children that you are going to read out twenty-four words, one at a time. Each word will be one of the tricky words that they have been learning. Tell the children that you will say the word, and then you will read out a sentence containing the word to help them remember what it means. You will then repeat the word on its own again before pausing so that the children can write the word down. For example: **busy**. I am very **busy**. **busy**

1. **busy**. I am very **busy**. **busy**
2. **people**. There were lots of **people** at the bus stop. **people**
3. **after**. I can have pudding **after** my dinner. **after**
4. **fast**. My brother can run **fast**. **fast**
5. **last**. I always arrive **last**. **last**
6. **past**. The **past** is what happened before. **past**
7. **father**. My **father** is a kind man. **father**
8. **class**. My **class** is called Oak. **class**
9. **grass**. I love the smell of freshly cut **grass**. **grass**
10. **pass**. I **pass** the ball. **pass**
11. **path**. The **path** was made from bricks. **path**
12. **bath**. I had a hot **bath**. **bath**
13. **hour**. An **hour** is sixty minutes. **hour**
14. **move**. We are going to **move** to a new house. **move**
15. **prove**. I want to **prove** my theory. **prove**
16. **improve**. I try to **improve** my handwriting. **improve**
17. **eye**. I have a sore **eye**. **eye**
18. **could**. We **could** watch television. **could**
19. **should**. We **should** read a book. **should**
20. **would**. I **would** like an apple. **would**
21. **who**. I don't know **who** is at the door. **who**
22. **clothes**. I hung up my clean **clothes**. **clothes**
23. **money**. I spent my **money**. **money**
24. **parents**. My **parents** work hard. **parents**

For those students who need a little more of a spelling challenge, read out the ten further 'Quiet Zone' words to spell: **sure**, **sugar**, **water**, **many**, **any**, **again**, **half**, **Mr**, **Mrs**, **Christmas**

Full details of how to carry out assessment can be found on pages 6 and 102 of this guide.

STATION - WEEK 30

High Speed

OBJECTIVES
Review
Spell and use words in writing from all Year 1 and Year 2 content

Review previous learning

Ask the children if they can recall the spelling content and any examples from the previous spelling lesson. Elicit ideas and remind the children that: They were learning about words that can be difficult to spell because the letter-sound correspondences in them have not yet been taught, but the words are so useful that we want to use them now.

Introducing the rule

Explain to the children that in today's lesson they will review words that contain spelling patterns taught in Year 1 and Year 2.

Pupil Book Activity 1: Write the words

1. Draw children's attention to the words in the boxes on page 60. Explain that all of these words contain spelling patterns that they learnt about in Year 1.
2. Ask the children to read through the words in the boxes and talk to a partner about what they mean. Then ask the children if there are any words they are unsure of and explain the meanings to them, looking in the dictionary for a definition if necessary.
3. Ask the children to copy each word in the boxes. Remind them to notice and think about the spelling patterns they have learnt.

Pupil Book Activity 2: Write the words

1. Draw children's attention to the words in the boxes on page 61. Explain that all of these words contain spelling patterns that they learnt about in Year 2.
2. Ask the children to read through the words in the boxes and talk to a partner about what they mean. Then ask the children if there are any words they are unsure of and explain the meanings to them, looking in the dictionary for a definition if necessary.
3. Ask the children to copy each word in the boxes. Remind them to notice and think about the spelling patterns they have learnt.

Assessment: High Speed Train review

All children should now be able to successfully participate in a rapid pace word assessment, which will enable you to quickly assess their progress and achievement through *Spelling Stations - Platform Two*. To do this, tell the children that you are going to call out lots of words, one at a time. Each word will be one of the review words that they have been practising. Tell the children that you will say the word then repeat it as they write it down.

KEEP YOUR TRAIN TOGETHER!

How 'High Speed' your train goes is best judged by you. Do remember that it is better to get your class to their destination steadily and in one piece, rather than go to quickly and leave some carriages behind!

1. miss	16. car	31. blue (colour)	46. unlock	61. brother
2. think	17. tree	32. grew	47. football	62. key
3. rocket	18. dream	33. pie	48. bridge	63. word
4. catch	19. bread	34. field	49. giraffe	64. warm
5. have	20. person	35. light	50. race	65. treasure
6. cats	21. summer	36. horse	51. circle	66. didn't
7. jumping	22. bird	37. yawn	52. knee	67. Tim's
8. fresher	23. turn	38. hair	53. gnome	68. station
9. rain	24. moon	39. beard	54. write (with a pen)	69. helpful
10. day	25. book	40. pear (fruit)	55. table	70. badly
11. made	26. boat	41. care	56. animal	71. watched
12. these	27. toes	42. happy	57. pencil	72. fastest
13. five	28. mouth	43. dolphin	58. cry	
14. home	29. brown	44. wheel	59. babies	
15. rule	30. snow	45. skin	60. walk	

Appendices

Assessment and Pupil Record Sheets 102-104
Spelling Certificate 105

Games & Activities 106-111
    Memory Trigger 106
    Attention Please! 107
    Lost Luggage! 108-109
    The Great Train Race! 110-111

Letterland Phonics 112-115
    What is Letterland Phonics? 112
    Scope of *Letterland Phonics Teacher's Guide* 113
    Abbreviated Letterland Phonics stories 114-115

Letterland Grammar 116-118
    What is Letterland Grammar? 116
    Scope of *Letterland Grammar Teacher's Guide* 117
    Abbreviated Letterland Grammar stories 118

Assessment

As part of your weekly routine (generally a Friday activity), spellings should be assessed. To stop this being 'the dreaded test', introduce the idea of **Spelling Stations!**

Each child should have a copy of *Spelling Stations Ticket Book - Platform Two*. Each week they will be tested on the words from **one ticket**. Children will have covered the spelling patterns in class in their *Pupil Book*. Children should be encouraged to revise the spellings in the *Ticket Book* at home with a parent/carer.

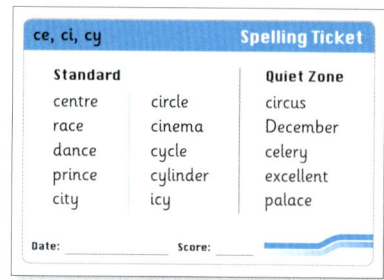

Procedure

Teacher: At the start of the spelling test, you could say: **"Spelling Stations - Tickets Please!"** Collect in the *Ticket Books*. You could blow a whistle to signify the start and end of the test.

Teacher: Read out the 'Standard' Word Bank and sentences from the Assessment section of the *Teacher's Guide* to the children slowly. Repeat.

Students: Write their test answers in their own exercise book, or on a separate sheet of paper.

Teacher: Read out the further 'Quiet Zone' words to spell for those in the class that need more of a spelling challenge. Remind the other children that they are in the 'Quiet Zone' and must stay quiet to help the other children concentrate.

Teacher: Collect all the student's answers to be marked.

Teacher: Mark the papers and keep a record of the spelling scores on the sheets provided on the next page or your own class record.

Teacher: Fill in the date (or use a date stamp) in each child's *Ticket Book* and their score. Return marked Spelling Tests to your students. Ask them to look at any errors they have made and write those words again in the space provided **on the back of their spelling ticket** so they (and their parents) have a record of how they are getting on with their spellings.

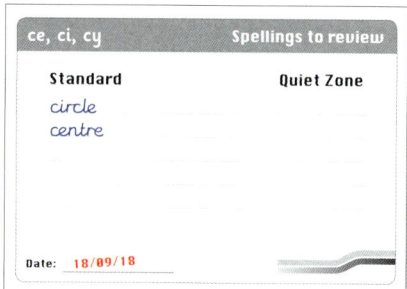

Differentiation

You will expect most students to learn the Standard list of 10-12 words per week, and the high achieving students to learn 15-18 words (both Standard and Quiet Zone). However you may discretely advise some students which portion of the list he or she is responsible for learning. For example, you could limit a student to only being expected to spell 5 Standard Words. They fully participate in class activities but are evaluated primarily on assigned words.

For students who are well below age-related expectations in reading and spelling, intervention at their instructional level is important.

Marking and scoring

- The Record Sheets overleaf are for Standard scores. Enter the total number of words spelt correctly.
- The target score for spelling is 80%.
- If a child is consistently scoring below 80%, colour the score boxes in red. Check if the student is fully understanding what is expected of them and whether they are doing any work at home to consolidate their learning. Encourage them to play the spelling games on pages 106-111. If scores continue to fall below the target, consider reducing the number of spellings per week and look to other intervention strategies, such as revisiting the phonic or grammatical structures using the *Letterland Phonics Teacher's Guide* or *Letterland Grammar Teacher's Guide* to ensure those foundations are fully formed.

Pupil Record Sheet 1

Letterland Spelling Stations Teacher's Guide - Platform 2

Name	Week														
	1	2	3	4	5	6	7	8	9	10	11	12	13	14	15
Andrew C	8/12	7/12	6/12	9/12	9/12										

© Letterland International 2018. May be photocopied only for use within purchasing school.

Pupil Record Sheet 2 Letterland **Spelling Stations Teacher's Guide - Platform 2**

Name	Week														
	16	17	18	19	20	21	22	23	24	25	26	27	28	29	30

© Letterland International 2018. May be photocopied only for use within purchasing school.

Letterland

Spelling Stations Award – Platform Two

This award is being presented to

_____

for completing all of the spellings set this year.

Keep up the good work!

Signed _____ Date _____

Letterland

Spelling Stations Award – Platform Two

This award is being presented to

_____

for completing all of the spellings set this year.

Keep up the good work!

Signed _____ Date _____

© Letterland International 2018. May be photocopied for use only within purchasing school.

Memory Trigger

The train station theme with memorable station names provides an association for the Word Banks. Each week has a station name and image associated with it. By remembering the station name, children have a visual clue to help them unlock the words of the week rather than simply remembering an abstract list of words.

Write a station name on the board, then invite children to come and add more words under each part of the station name using the same spelling patterns. See how long your lists can grow!

Knitted Gnomes

knit	gnat
knight	gnash
knot	gnarled

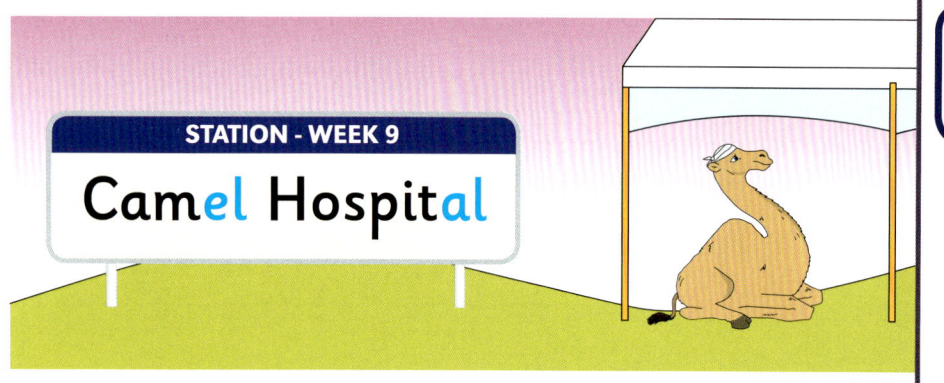

Camel Hospital

towel	metal
travel	pedal
cancel	capital
jewel	medal

Small Stall

fall	call
wall	tall
ball	hall

Attention Please!

Number of players: Whole class split into teams (minimum 4 per team.) Children should be arranged so that groups can't see each others' pages.

Children need: Paper pencil and an eraser.

Preparation: Give the groups about 15 seconds to decide on a team name. Those that can't agree can be assigned a colour or number instead. Let someone from each group write their team name on the board for score-keeping.

How to play

The teacher leads the activity. Pretend you are in a station reading a station announcement. Children will not get the full announcement – just parts of it. The announcement gives clues to a mystery word from the Word Bank for the week. Children must guess the word and spell it correctly, agreeing on the word and spelling within their group. The teacher moves around the room to check answers.

- The teacher says one clue at a time. The first clue should be general enough to relate to a few of the words the children have learnt that week. Clues may relate to spelling, word structure or meaning. For example, for Week 23, you could say:

  "Attention please! This word starts with the letter l."

- After you give the first clue, the children within each group can whisper together and guess what they think it is. Their group must write one word down (either they can all write the same word on individual papers or they can choose a scribe for the group).

- The teacher walks around looking over children's shoulders. If a group have the correct word and it is spelt correctly, the teacher sends one group member to the board to record points (4 points for the correct word on first clue).

- If a group doesn't have the correct word spelt correctly, the teacher says something like: **"Good try, but not the word I am thinking of,"** or: **"That looks like it might be the right word, but that is not the correct spelling"**. The group crosses out the word and waits for the next announcement.

- If a group cannot agree upon a word, the teacher can call: **"Time's up!"** and go on to the next clue.

- The teacher gives a second clue: **"Attention please! This word has the suffix –ly on the end"**.

- Groups who have not 'scored' try again. Teacher gives feedback as above. (3 points for the correct word on second clue).

- Teacher gives a third clue.

  "Attention please! This word means something or somebody is very pleasant."

- A meaning clue is generally easiest. (2 points for the correct word on third clue).

  Finally, if some groups still do not have the correct word, spelt correctly, the teacher says the word, **"lovely"** and everyone writes it (including groups who have already received points).

- Follow the same steps with as many words as you have time for.

Winning

The group with the most points wins!

Badgers	Queens	Tigers
4 2	2	2 2
Elfs	Blues	Clever Cats
2 3	3	
Unicorns	Kings	Reds
	3 2	2 4

Lost Luggage!

Number of players: Whole class can play in groups of two or three.

Children need: *Spelling Ticket* for the Week, Lost Luggage gameboard (page 109).

Preparation: Using the *Spelling Ticket* for one or two weeks, find the words with more than one syllable. Write the syllables of each word on the bags - one syllable per bag, spread randomly around the board. Try and fill all the bags.
Note: This game works best on those weeks that have a number of two/three syllable words, see example below.

How to play

Swap pages with another player. One player says "Go." Both players start trying to find syllables that make a word, writing that word on the line below. Tick off and/or join the bags as you use them. Each bag can only be used once. To win you have to use all the syllables to make words from the Word Bank. You may need to change some words if you have syllables left over at the end that do not form a word.

Winning

When a player has finished, he or she shouts "Luggage Found!," and turns their paper over. That player may not change any answers after that. The other player continues until they are finished.

Players then swap papers. They check each others' answers to make sure that all syllables have been used and only used once. They must also check for correct spelling. If there are no errors, the player that finished first wins. If there are errors, the player with fewest errors wins.

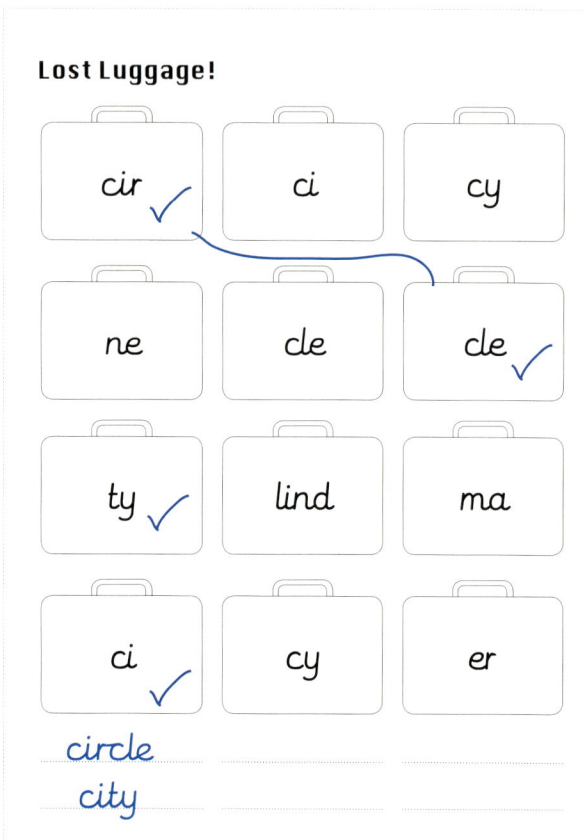

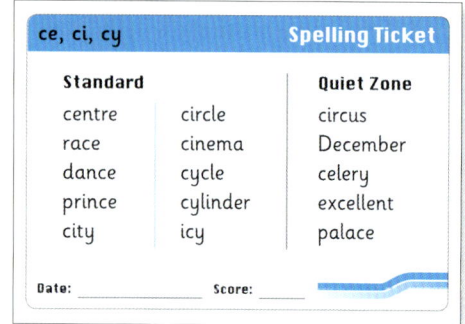

Lost Luggage!

The Great Train Race!

Number of players: This game can be played in small groups or by individuals.

Children need: The Great Train Race! gameboard (page 111, laminated or placed in a plastic protector) and a die.

How to play

Writing out words again and again to memorise them can get a bit dull. So this game is specifically designed to allow children to practise five words they are finding challenging, but in a fun way. You could assign specific words to each child, or ask them to choose words written on the back of their *Spelling Tickets,* as they will all be spellings that the children need to review.

Each child writes down five words next to numbers 1-5 in a list. Make sure they have this list as they play the game. The game aims to encourage them to write the words lots of times, not to test them.

As they throw the die they write the word that corresponds to the number in the space provided. If they throw a six, they miss a turn. Children can race against themselves (against the clock) or someone else. Which colour train will get to the finish first?

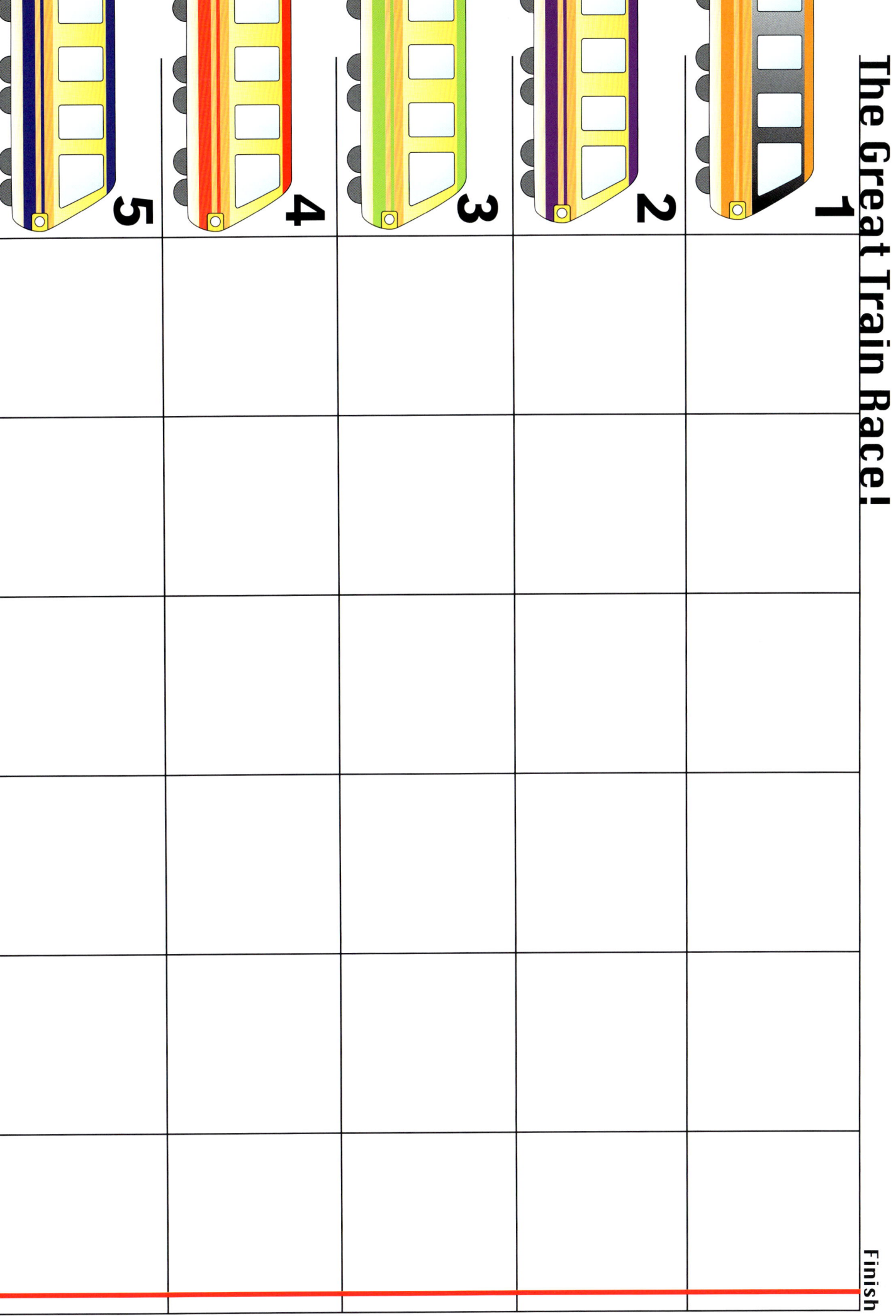

What is Letterland Phonics?

Letterland is a unique, phonics-based approach to teaching reading, writing and spelling to 3-8 year olds. Its characters make plain black letter shapes and their sounds easy and fun to remember. They give speedy access to **all 44 sounds and their major spellings**. They create fast, smooth transitions to blending plain letters to read, and segmenting spoken words to spell.

How does it work?

Sounds
Harry Hat Man makes the sound at the beginning of his name. Just whisper it – '**hhh...**'.

Shapes
Hurry from the Hat Man's head down to his heel on the ground.
Go up and bend his knee over, so he'll hop while he makes his sound.

Actions
Actions for each letter create strong multisensory cues for quickly learning and recalling letter shapes and sounds.

Uppercase
When Harry has a chance to start a name, he is so happy, he does a handstand with his hat on!

Digraphs
Whenever Sammy Snake starts to hiss loudly behind Harry Hat Man, the Hat Man turns back and says '**sh!**' because he hates noise.

Letterland activates every learning channel through simple phonics-related stories, actions, songs and activities.

1. **Learn letter sounds**

   Once you have met the friendly Letterland characters, just start to say their names for the correct letter sound.

2. **Learn letter shapes**

   Simple rhymes and songs about the Letterland characters ensure correct letter formation, avoiding confusion over similar looking letters.

3. **Word building**

   Blending and segmenting words is introduced very early on, covering blends, digraphs and trigraphs.

4. **Advanced spelling**

   Phonics stories give children a friendly logic for remembering all 44 letter sounds and their major spellings.

5. **Full literacy**

   Letterland takes children through from the very first foundation stages of learning to full literacy with a wide range of resources; from flashcards and software to decodable readers and handwriting resources. To find out more about the range, please visit our website: www.letterland.com

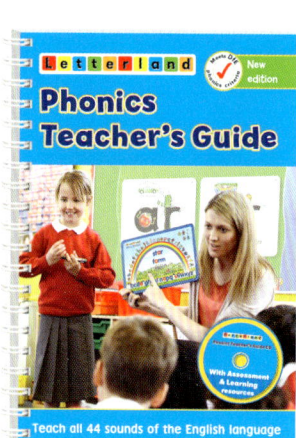

Scope of Letterland Phonics Teacher's Guide

Section 1: Fast Track - Phonemic Awareness

Teaching Focus:
- An alphabet immersion activity introducing all **a-z** shapes and their sounds
- Developing phonemic awareness of beginning sounds in words

Assessment Objective:
- Say the sound when shown the plain letter (21 consonants and 5 short vowels)
- Sort pictured words according to initial sound

Section 2: a-z Word Building

Teaching Focus:
- **a-z** letters in detail (uppercase/lowercase)
- First blending and segmenting (after six letters)
- Introducing long vowels while keeping the focus of Word Building on short vowels
- Common consonant digraphs: **ch ck sh th th ng**
- Introducing a limited number of 'tricky' words
- Practising decoding and reading 'tricky' words in brief, engaging stories

Assessment Objective:
- Say the sound(s) when shown the plain letter(s) for 21 consonants, 5 short and long vowels, 5 consonant digraphs
- Write the letter(s) in response to the sound
- Recognise uppercase and lowercase letter forms
- Blend and segment VC and CVC words
- Spell regular VC and CVC words accurately
- Read 21 'tricky' words
- Read decodable text with adequate comprehension

Section 3: Blending with Adjacent Consonants

Teaching Focus:
- Initial adjacent consonants:
  sc sk sp st sm sn sw
  bl cl fl gl pl sl
  br cr dr fr gr pr tr
- Final adjacent consonants: **-st -sk -nd -nt -nk**

Assessment Objective:
- Blend and segment words of four sounds
- Read stories with adjacent consonant words
- Blend and segment CCVC and CVCC words
- Read 9 additional 'tricky' words (cumulative total: 30)
- Read decodable text containing adjacent consonants and 'tricky' words with accuracy, fluency and comprehension

Section 4: Long Vowels

Teaching Focus:
- **y** with long **i** sound (as in sk**y**)
  y with long **e** sound (as in bab**y**)
- Split digraphs: **a_e e_e i_e o_e u_e**
- Suffix: **ed** with three sounds /ed/ /d/ /t/
- Vowel digraphs: **ai ay ee ea ie oa ue**
- Long vowel spellings: **ind ild old**
- Blending and segmenting long vowel words
- Reading stories with long vowel words and also recognising 'tricky' words

Assessment Objective:
- Say the sound of split digraphs and long vowel digraphs when shown the plain letters
- Say three sounds for **y** and three for **-ed** when shown the plain letters
- Blend and segment words with long vowels
- Decode words with suffix **-ed**
- Read 17 new 'tricky' words (cumulative total: 47)
- Read decodable text containing long vowel words with accuracy, fluency and comprehension

Section 5: Further Vowel Sounds and Spellings

Teaching Focus:
- R-controlled vowels: **ar or er ir ur air ear**
- Long vowel patterns: **ow igh**
- Other vowel sounds: **oo oo u** (in push) **ou ow oi oy aw au ew**
- Reading stories with all the new sounds

Assessment Objective:
- Say the new sound when shown the letters
- Blend and segment words with the various vowel patterns and sounds
- Read 21 new 'tricky' words (cumulative total: 68)
- Apply the new sounds in reading with increasing accuracy, fluency and comprehension

Combining Letterland Spelling and Letterland Phonics

Letterland Spelling Teacher's Guide can be used in conjunction with the *Letterland Phonics Teacher's Guide* to cover all your curriculum requirements. Children may have already covered a lot of phonics in their reception year, but there are those who may be struggling to remember some of what they have covered. Finding a new way to present the information, using a new learning channel and engaging children with stories and characters, can be the key to successfully advancing the whole class.

The following pages give just the abbreviated stories about the Letterland characters and how they interact with each other to create a memorable way to learn and remember phonics. For full stories and teaching techniques please refer to the *Phonics Teacher's Guide* and accompanying product range.

Visit www.letterland.com for more details.

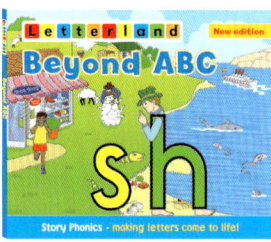
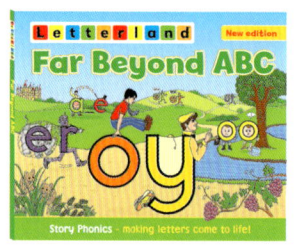
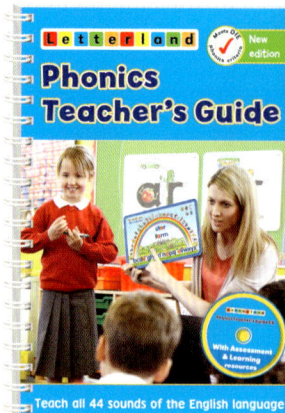

3: Huge Bridge	–ge		cage hinge vegetables	Blue Magic lights up Gentle Ginger.
	–dge		badge bridge edge	Dippy Duck is dazzled and silent next to Gentle Gingle the Gymnast and Blue Magic **e**
4: Magic Gym	gi		giant imagine magic	Blue Magic lights up Gentle Ginger, the Gymnast.
	gy		Egypt energy spongy	Blue Magic lights up Gentle Ginger, the Gymnast.
5: Ice City	ce		fence office scenery	Clever Cat turns into a hissing snake before a nice, Blue Magic **e**.
	ci		city pencil science	Clever Cat turns into a hissing snake before Blue Magic **i**.
	cy		bicycle cylinder secrecy	Clever Cat turns into a hissing snake before Blue Magic **y**.
6: Knitted Gnome	kn		knee knife unknown	Kicking King stays quiet next to Noisy Nick.
7: Wrinkly Writer	wr		wrist write wrong	Red Robot captures Walter in his sack. Walter is too startled to speak.

8: Little Apples	le		Sparks shooting: ab<u>le</u>, tab<u>le</u>, brid<u>le</u> Sparks blocked: app<u>le</u>, rid<u>dle</u>, hob<u>ble</u>	Candle Magic changes Lucy into a Magic candle.
9: Camel Hospital	al			Parachuted apples land with a thud and say 'uh'.
11: Dry July	y		fl<u>y</u> m<u>y</u> tr<u>y</u>	Yellow Yo-yo Man gets a great big free ice cream from Mr I for taking his place and saying 'I!' for him.
12: Baby Bunnies	–y to –ies		cry/cr<u>ies</u> happy/happ<u>iest</u>	The Yo-yo Man changes from his working clothes into his **i**-clothes whenever **-es**, **-ed**, **-er**, **-est** or any other ending can finish the words for him. (Exception: the **-ing** ending.)
15: Humming Runner	Best friends		ru<u>nn</u>er pa<u>tt</u>ing sto<u>pp</u>ing	Best friends love making their sound together and blocking magic sparks. There are lots of Best Friends in Letterland.
17: Small Stall	al all		<u>al</u>most <u>al</u>so <u>al</u>ways b<u>all</u> c<u>all</u> h<u>all</u>	Giant All sometimes pulls a word up beside him and leans on it so we can only see one of his legs. Don't expect to hear the usual 'a' sound as Giant All eats almost all the apples he can find!
18: Honey Love	o		s<u>o</u>n l<u>o</u>ve m<u>o</u>nth	Oscar's bothersome little brother is too little to say 'o' like Oscar. So he just says 'uh'.
19: Donkey Valley	–ey		journ<u>ey</u> donk<u>ey</u> monk<u>ey</u>	When these two men go out on a journey together, Mr E does the talking and the Yo-yo Man is the Lookout Man.
23: Lovely Refreshment	–ly		bad<u>ly</u> love<u>ly</u> prompt<u>ly</u>	Lucy and the Yo-yo Man together say 'lee' in over 4000 words.
24: Careful! Darkness!	–ful		pain<u>ful</u> rest<u>ful</u> wonder<u>ful</u>	Giant Full sometimes pulls a word up beside him and leans on it so we can only see one of his legs.
27: Action Station	–tion		conversa<u>tion</u> explana<u>tion</u> informa<u>tion</u>	Mr 'Tion's trick is to remember the phrase **T**ea **I O**we **N**ick.

What is Letterland Grammar?

The emphasis of *Letterland Grammar* is on the ways in which children's writing can be improved by using simple grammatical concepts.
It is a journey of exploration. Giving a child an analogy they can relate to has always been the key to Letterland's success. In the same way as the Letterland characters help children to learn phonics and letter shapes, *Letterland Grammar* uses analogies to explain grammatical concepts.

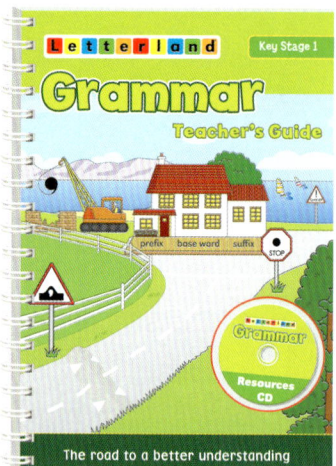

Most children have travelled in cars or buses, travelled down different types of streets and seen lots of different types of buildings. They will have noticed road signs and may know that these tell the driver something about the road. If we relate this analogy to reading, we can describe stories as towns. Within those towns there are streets which we call sentences. The words we see are the buildings, and just as buildings are modified, extended or developed, so words can change with the addition of prefixes, suffixes and tenses. With *Letterland Grammar*, as a child is reading, they are encouraged to think of their finger as a car travelling along a street looking out for 'reading' signs along the way.

Combining Letterland Spelling and Letterland Grammar

Letterland Grammar covers the statutory requirements laid out in the National Curriculum for English at Key Stage 1 (England) for both Year 1 and Year 2.

The structure of the guide is based on concepts rather than year group. This enables you to teach the concepts in a flexible way, and at the pace best suited to individual children and classes. The pages that follow give you a brief summary of the analogies used in *Letterland Grammar*. Just imagine your Spelling train pulling in at the Grammar town and link the programmes together!
For full details of the programme, please visit www.letterland.com

Scope of Letterland Grammar Teacher's Guide

Unit & Chapter	Topic	Definition
1.1	**Capital letter** **Full stop**	A sign to show where a sentence starts. A sign to show where a sentence ends.
1.2	**Question mark**	A sign to show the end of a sentence that is a question.
1.3	**Exclamation mark**	A sign to show the end of a sentence. It indicates surprise, shock or excitement in direct speech.
1.4	**Commas for lists**	A sign used to separate items in a list or series.
1.5a	**Apostrophe - possessive**	A mark above the text before a final **s** to identify the owner of something.
1.5b	**Apostrophe - contraction**	A mark showing the place where one or more letters and their sounds have been deleted to shorten a word.
2.1	**Conjunction - and**	A 'joining word', used to link words, phrases or clauses in a sentence.
2.2	**Coordinating conjunction** **Subordinating conjunction**	A 'joining word', used to join words, phrases or clauses that are of equal importance within a sentence. Used to link a main and a dependent clause.
2.3	**Expanded noun phrase**	A group of words that work together to give information about the noun.
2.4	**Statements, questions exclamations, commands**	Sentences which tell you something, end with a question mark, an exclamation mark, or tell you to do something.
3.1	**Plural noun suffix**	Suffixes (letters joined to the end of a word) that turn a noun, meaning one thing, into a noun meaning two or more things.
3.2	**Suffixes added to verbs**	Suffixes can be added to verbs with no change to the root verb. Verbs are words about 'doing' something.
3.3	**Prefix**	A group of letters joined to the beginning of a word to change its meaning.
3.4	**Suffixes to form nouns**	A group of letters joined to the end of a word (some change to the root word) to change its meaning and make a noun.
3.5	**Compound noun**	A noun that is made by joining two or more words, e.g. noun+noun, adjective+noun, verb+noun.
3.6/3.7	**Suffixes to form adjectives**	A group of letters joined to the end of a word to change its meaning and make an adjective.
3.8	**Suffixes to form adverbs**	A group of letters joined to the end of a word to change its meaning and make an adverb.
4.1	**Present and past tense**	The form of a verb that shows when something happens, past or present.
4.2	**Present progressive and past tense**	The form of a verb that shows a continuing action in the past or present, created by adding a form of the verb 'to be'.

Combining *Letterland Spelling* and *Letterland Grammar*

In the *Letterland Spelling Stations Teacher's Guide* you will cover some suffixes, prefixes and compound nouns. The aim of each lesson is to introduce the pattern and use Word Banks to embed those spellings in the minds of your students. To introduce grammatical concepts, such as suffixes and prefixes, you may find it useful to use the *Grammar Teacher's Guide* alongside your spelling programme.

The abbreviated stories of concepts you will encounter in the *Spelling Stations Teacher's Guide - Platform Two* can be found below. For more information please visit www.letterland.com.

12: Baby Bunnies	**Plural noun suffix**	A suffix is like an extension added to the side of a house.	
14: Stripy Hiker 15: Humming Runner 15: Careful! Darkness!	**Suffixes added to verbs** **Suffixes to form adjectives**	A suffix is like an extension added to the side of a building. A verb is like a building where there are things happening; like a factory or office building.	
13: Happy Happier 23: Lovely Refreshment	**Suffixes to form adverbs**	There are lots of different types of extensions to buildings, just as there are different suffixes.	
17: Small Stall	**Prefixes**	A prefix is like a porch that we add to the front of a house or building.	
25: Don't run!	**Apostrophe - contraction**	An apostrophe of contraction is like a demolition ball. It shows that letters (sounds) have been knocked away like bricks.	
26: Tom's Ticket	**Apostrophe - possessive**	An apostrophe of possession is like the speech bubble of a person on a roof-top of a building, shouting out, "It belongs to me!".	

NOTE: The *Grammar Teacher's Guide* also contains brief lesson plans for the Letterland phonics character stories for the following prefixes and suffixes:

Prefix *al*– (Giant All)

Suffix –*ful* (Giant Full)

Suffixes –*en*, –*est* (Magic Endings)

Doubling consonants (Best Friends to the Rescue)

Suffix –*le* (Candle Magic)

Suffixes –*ible*, –*able* (Burnt out candles)

Suffix –*ly* (Lucy Lamp Light and Yellow Yo-yo Man)

Suffix –*tion* (Mr 'Tion)

Suffix –*ture* (Talking Tess sneezes)

y to *i* (Yellow Yo-yo Man changes into **i**-clothes)

More stories - Abbreviated lore for further suffixes –*al*, –*cy*, –*gy*, –*ous*, –*rry*